BY HEATHER WAGNER

Friend or FAUX

a guide to fussy vegans, crazy cat ladies, creepy clingers, undercover sluts, and other girls who will quietly *destroy* your life

QUIRK BOOKS
PHILADELPHIA

Copyright © 2009 by Quirk Productions, Inc.

Library of Congress Cataloging in Publication Number: 2008937681

ISBN: 978-1-59474-320-7

Printed in Singapore
Typeset in Wendy LP, New Century Schoolbook, and Univers

Edited by Mindy Brown
Designed by Jenny Kraemer
Illustrations © Monika Melnychuk / i2iart
Production management by John J. McGurk

Distributed in North America by Chronicle Books
680 Second Street
San Francisco, CA 94107

10 9 8 7 6 5 4 3 2 1

Quirk Books
215 Church Street
Philadelphia, PA 19106
www.quirkbooks.com

contents

threat level green: The No-Risk Friend

contents

threat level blue: The Low-Risk Friend

contents

threat level yellow: The Moderate-Risk Friend

threat level orange: The High-Risk Friend

contents

threat level red: The Severe-Risk Friend

introduction

From your best friend on the monkey bars to the woman who swears you don't need Botox, friends are fundamental to the female experience. They're your confidantes, your sisters, your "rocks." You all saw *Beaches* and you all cried—and not just because of Bette Midler's shoulder pads and frizzy orange mane. Friendship is the ultimate support system in an unstable world: Men are unreliable. Family forgives too much, or too little. Booze is caloric. But our girlfriends give us strength, validation, and much-needed fashion advice.

And yet there are likely a few friends in your circle who pose exceptions to this rule. Ladies who may appear to have your best intentions at heart but are actually, upon close inspection, pure evil.

We're always warned of "the bad boy," but what about "the bad girl"? The friend who smiles sweetly as she flirts with your boyfriend, shrugs as she takes credit for your work, belittles you with such a soft touch you don't realize it's happening until she saunters away and you find yourself in need of a big box of chocolate-covered Xanax?

There are guides for how to get a man, how to marry a man, how to dump a man, how to deal with a man who's dumped you, but not so much about that other, oftentimes more profound relationship. This book profiles friends on all points of the Friend–Frenemy spectrum, from the steadfast to the skanky, and spurs you to take action—whether it's to run like hell or to keep and cherish her.

As in the classic Girl Scouts campfire tune, true friends may be either silver or gold. But in the pages that follow you'll see that some are made up of more sinister materials. Like pleather.

Friend or Faux is more than just a collection of "types." *Much* more! This tome also provides you with a plan of action for each friend profiled. Do you give her time or give her the boot? Just reference the "What to do" category that accompanies each entry and you'll be ready for action (or calculated inaction)!

Additionally, the simple color-coded Friend Threat Level system will alert you to the relative dangers and emotional hazards of every friend profiled, making this book your own personal Department of Homegirl Security.

threat level green
The No-Risk Friend

Although their assigned color is green, these friends are
true blue! Kind, empathetic, endlessly forgiving, and
essential to your well-being, these are your steadfast
pals-for-life. Sure, they have their quirks. But they've
always got your back.

the late-to-the-party friend

HABITAT: California Pizza Kitchen, cover band shows, Pashmina stores

IDENTIFYING CHARACTERISTICS: Logo fabric, Appeltini,
  "The Rachel" haircut

PROS: Reminds you that 1999 was kind of awesome

CONS: Refuses to IM; says "biatch" a lot

CATCHPHRASE: "Cosmos all 'round!"

It's easy to identify the Late-to-the-Party Friend. Set your cell phone ringer to "Gold Digger." Wait. The squeal of joy and immediate "rap dance" pantomime will say it all. Or she'll ask you if you've ever heard of this thing called "YouTube" and then forward you "Dick in a Box" with a subject header that reads: HILARIOUS!!!!☺ On her bulky Magnavox TV you'll find episodes of *Survivor* and *Alias* recorded—like magic—by this newfangled gadget called "TiVo." The Late-to-the-Party Friend can be refreshing in that she will react with wide-eyed wonder at your grasp of basic celebrity couplings and young starlet meltdowns. "Since when did Nick and Jessica break up?" she may wail with sincere dismay. "They seemed so happy together!" As such, she may actually have insightful opinions on things like philosophy, literature, relationships, and the greater part of "reality" not limited to reality shows.

WHAT TO DO

You have just found the last person in the free world who hasn't seen a celebrity v-g shot. Hold on to her.

the smart ditzy friend

HABITAT: Traffic school, locked outside her apartment, the wrong Italian restaurant on the wrong night

IDENTIFYING CHARACTERISTICS: Big smile, flawless hair, skirt on backward

PRO: Is bubbly and charming

CON: Asks you if Algeria is better than Benadryl

CATCHPHRASE: "No. Really? No. Really?"

The Smart Ditzy Friend is the inspiration behind every dumb blonde joke ever told. But though she may appear spacey, she's actually quite sharp. She may have a master's degree or be a VP somewhere, it's just that sometimes the details, the obvious, or the correct spelling of "sincerely" elude her. Who knows if she's playing it up to put herself at an advantage—after all, it never hurts to be underestimated by one's peers—or if it's a genuine series of mental lapses. All you know is that it's hilarious. Like the time she picked up a bottle of fancy department store moisturizer that billed itself as a "refreshment for the skin" and asked, in all earnestness, if you're supposed to drink it. Or when she bid farewell to her new pals on a trip to Mexico with a hearty, "Muchos Noches!" Usually guys find her adorable, a brazenly bubble-headed Chrissy in a world of pragmatic Janets. And let's face it, so do you.

WHAT TO DO

Keep close tabs on her, and try to tone down your incredulous laughter.

the hot asian friend

HABITAT: Thomas Keller restaurants, Côte D'Azur, design studio

IDENTIFYING CHARACTERISTICS: Exquisitely slim, shiny magical hair, fancy purse

PRO: Is a cheap date

CON: Makes you feel like a dude

CATCHPHRASE: "Next time we're going to the *real* sushi place."

The Hot Asian Friend is so hot, in such a specific physiological way, that she presents zero threat to you. You can bask in second-hand attention without feeling any grumpy pangs of jealousy. The genetic lottery has blessed her with perfect bone structure, so she needn't obsess over the trivialities of self-image; instead she has a quiet confidence and savoir faire, to say nothing of her advanced ability to deflect unwanted male attention—of which there will be plenty. The Hot Asian Friend either has a loving, devoted boyfriend or a loving, devoted husband, and in rare periods of singledom she instantly accrues a coterie of male suitors who buy her jewelry and cause her very little emotional trauma. As such, the time you usually spend talking a friend off the ledge after another jerky guy has decided he "needs space" is spent discussing other matters—including, yes, you!

WHAT TO DO

Be sure to keep her away from any guy friends who've announced they have an "Asian fetish." Those guys are losers anyhow.

shiny magical hair

air of quiet confidence

perfect bone structure

exquisitely slim

fancy purse

the stoner friend

HABITAT: The couch

IDENTIFYING CHARACTERISTICS: Unwashed hair, loopy grin, the same jeans since last Tuesday

PRO: Is mellow and fun

CON: Isn't so good at dispensing advice, remembering your birthday, or critical thinking

CATCHPHRASE: "What? Oh."

Stoner Friend is a preferred companion because her mood is consistent. You'll never witness her in a bitchy freakout or fit of rage over a parking ticket. She asks you basic questions and then seems really interested in your response, sometimes following up with an observation that be maybe a bit off-topic but a lot more intellectually stimulating than, say, The Magic Sparkle Pegasus Powder Friend, who just asks, repeatedly, if you know where the after-party is. Stoner Friend is great to watch movies with, although she will likely only want to watch the same titles over and over, absorbed in the obvious. (Like how Russell Crowe is just saying the lines. He's not *really* the Gladiator. He's just acting right now.) But sometimes her commentary will run more to the non sequitur and profound: "What if you had a heart attack and died on a plane, but at the same time crossed the international dateline? Then you'd be alive . . . in the future." Now try going to sleep.

WHAT TO DO

Chillax with your Stoner Friend, and assure her that yes, the pizza is on its way.

the mature friend
(AKA THE MOM FRIEND)

HABITAT: Adult women's choral group, Nordstrom's "Savvy" section

IDENTIFYING CHARACTERISTICS: Pencil skirt, nice watch, poise

PRO: Takes care of everything

CON: Makes you feel juvenile and bratty

CATCHPHRASE: "It's probably time for me to call it a night."

The Mature Friend is always calm, in control, and just this side of maternal. She discreetly slips you $20 for a cab when you leave your debit card at the bar. Which bar? You can't remember, but she'll give you a ride in her reliable Volvo once you finally do. She lives alone, with shabby-chic furnishings and a well-tended herb garden. When you come over for margaritas, she'll pour your proffered Tostitos into a ceramic bowl and quietly put your Cuervo in a cupboard, presenting you with top-shelf Hornitas, freshly squeezed lime, and rock-salt-rimmed hand-blown glasses she got in Oaxaca. Her style is conservative and exudes pure elegance, and while you often wonder why you can't be more like her, sometimes you think, on your fifth margarita, that if she took more risks, she'd learn a thing or two about life! Then she announces that she needs to call it a night because she has a Curves class in the morning, and your point goes unexpressed. It's probably a good thing.

WHAT TO DO

Return her many favors and be sure to compliment her Longchamp mom-purse.

the tan friend

HABITAT: Beach, park bench, tanning bed

IDENTIFYING CHARACTERISTICS: Bandeau top, freckles, slick lotiony skin

PRO: Looks sun-kissed and glowy

CON: And slightly cancerous

CATCHPHRASE: "Yo, it's PTH!" (prime tanning hours)

The Tan Friend has no recognizable goal in life other than to be tan. As long as her skin is the color of a roasted almond, all is right with the world. As a young girl, she may have experimented with aluminum foil and cooking oils when Hawaiian Tropic Deep Tan just wasn't reflective enough. And into her teens and twenties, when the rest of your friends were slathering on progressively higher SPFs, she went commando, a practice she liked to call "power tanning." She tries to keep things up in the winter (lean in, and you're likely to catch an unmistakable coconut-and-radiation scent). A master alchemist, she is also adept at mixing various bronzing sprays, powders, and lotions to further augment her tone. But when summer comes, all bets are off. She will likely be an entirely different race by August. You'll feel a little pasty by comparison, but the good vibes and sheer audacity of her SPF-shunning wiles are an intoxicatingly positive force.

WHAT TO DO

Bask in her glow. Sure, she may look like a withered old bag by the time she hits 35, but for now, shine on Tan Friend!

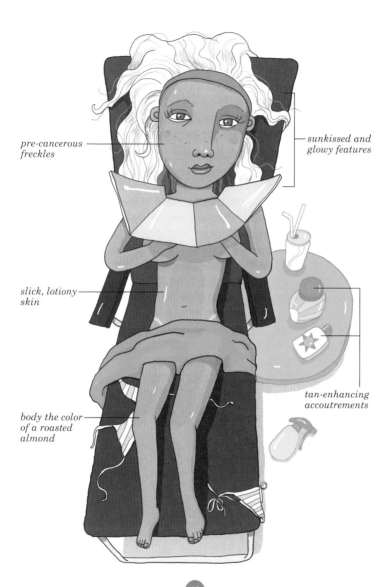

pre-cancerous freckles

sunkissed and glowy features

slick, lotiony skin

tan-enhancing accoutrements

body the color of a roasted almond

the crisis neutralizer friend

HABITAT: On her way over!

IDENTIFYING CHARACTERISTICS: Soothing earth tones

PRO: Makes you feel better about everything, instantly

CON: Lets you get away with murder

CATCHPHRASE: "Relax, everything's going to be fine."

The Crisis Neutralizer is equal parts politician, hostage negotiator, and MacGyver-style problem solver. She is able to get you to see the bright side of any issue, talks you off the ledge when things are going poorly, and has the uncanny ability to both soothe and amuse, like Cookie Monster, only without the crazed chocolate chip binges. She might be a child of a particularly nasty divorce, or the eldest sibling in a boisterous family; either way, she learned from a young age that, for the most part, people just want to be reassured, even if it means lying to them. She is the one person you call when you wake up at 6 A.M. in some random dude's apartment wearing only a large white undershirt. She will talk you through the steps that will get you home, to the Burger King, or to the pharmacy for emergency contraception, depending on the severity of the encounter. She will assure you that it's not a big deal and that you're still a good person with solid morals. Which you are!

WHAT TO DO

Keep her on speed dial. Everything's going to be OK.

the artsy friend

HABITAT: Obscure galleries, specialty paint store, in the studio

IDENTIFYING CHARACTERISTICS: Simple paint-stained clothes, canvas bag, no makeup

PRO: Lives for Art

CON: Is esoteric and confusing

CATCHPRHASE: "I've been thinking a lot about foam lately."

Despite her prohibitive moniker, Artsy Friend can be a wonderful pal to have. You frame her birthday cards and cherish her sensitivity and depth. She is unobtrusive and humble, and even if you get the sense she's some sort of crazy genius, she never uses her talent as social capital. She'll mumble that she's going to miss your housewarming party because she'll be "out of town," which only after lengthy questioning reveals itself to be a summer program at the Sorbonne. Artsy Friend has such a rich interior life that real-world interacting can be difficult. When you bring her to a seemingly manageable gathering, like a backyard cookout, she's more content to examine the way the light plays off the butane tank than to make pleasant, frivolous small talk. Guys may be put off, thinking she's weird or hostile, but just bait her with a few questions about pastoral imagery in Northern European painting, and you'll suddenly have a cultured chatterbox on your hands.

WHAT TO DO

Tailor your interactions to one-on-one activities,
as opposed to keggers.

the armchair psychologist friend

HABITAT: Self-help aisle

IDENTIFYING CHARACTERISTICS: Cute glasses, aura of deep understanding, box of tissues

PRO: Free therapy!

CON: Does she know too much?

CATCHPHRASE: "Mm-hmm. Tell me more about that."

The Armchair Psychologist is the friend to go to when you have a problem. Which is pretty much all the time. She will sit you down on her overstuffed couch, pour you a cup of mint tea, lean back with hands in her lap, and say, "OK. Talk." You spill all your neuroses, and she'll pause for a moment, regarding the ceiling. And then she'll issue a statement that immediately makes you feel either 100 percent better or 100 percent ready to jump off the bridge. (Keep in mind: The Armchair Psychologist does not filter her advice through a best-case-scenario lens, like your Crisis Neutralizer Friend.) She's likely to say, "I think this man is not ready for a serious relationship and you should move on." But wait, you say. I loooove him! She will then shrug and say that you may just have a sentimental attachment to the "idea" of him, and then ask you about your Dad. Providing you with a sweet, sweet distraction that is therapeutic in and of itself.

WHAT TO DO

Indulge in her super-human listening skills, but try not to refer to your time spent together as a "session."

the party-times foreign friend

HABITAT: Espresso bar, Internet café, the pub

IDENTIFYING CHARACTERISTICS: Multilingual, smokes everywhere, drinks her weight in lager

PRO: Open to all experiences; so friendly, so cultured!

CON: You don't know what the hell she's saying half the time

CATCHPHRASE: "Ees fabulous!"

You met the Party-Times Foreign Friend on one of those summer backpacky jaunts to Europe. Inevitably, you got sick of your back-packing buddies and headed out solo to experience "the real [insert European city]." You found yourself sitting at a pub or café, trying to look blasé and un-American, when Party-Times Foreign Friend bounded up and asked if you wanted to join her, and you ended up having the craziest night ever! You became fast friends, and whenever she visits it's like a breath of fresh, if Gauloise-scented, air. She doesn't do irony, isn't petty or shallow, can party all night, and is usually accompanied by a leather-clad but affable foreign boyfriend who says nothing but pays for everything. Under her tutelage, you learn Estonian swear words and master the art of the non-awkward double-cheek kiss. Your other friends may view her with quizzical consternation, but screw them and their narrow-minded provincial banality. You're going to the discothèque!

WHAT TO DO

Cherish your across-the-pond pal. *Vive la différence*!

the Texan friend

HABITAT: Dallas, Houston, Austin, sometimes El Paso

IDENTIFYING CHARACTERISTICS: Can-do spirit, Daisy Dukes, hook 'em horns gesture

PRO: Fun! Spunky! Hospitable!

CON: Are the pigtails *really* necessary?

CATCHPHRASE: "I did not just say *y'all*, y'all!"

You can take the Texan Friend out of the Lone Star state but . . . well, let's just say everything about her is redolent of big sky, oil rigs, men in boots, and upscale steakhouses. She is exuberant, family-oriented, and often sentimental about Texas, which you'll soon come to realize is an entirely different planet with its own particular social codes and vernacular. She'll say, "I'm fixin' to go!" when she's restless; "Just a woofin' ya" when she's making a light-hearted joke at your expense. The term "Coke" is a blanket term for all carbonated beverages. She is wonderful at making people feel at ease, but her warm-heartedness can sometimes be off-putting for jaded urbanites accustomed to a bit more brittleness. She has strong opinions about gun control and BBQ and is very much into things that kick ass. Texas, you'll learn, kicks much ass. Delaware . . . not so much.

WHAT TO DO

Always compliment her brisket, and remember that when she says, "Y'all are some good people!" she's referring to you, singular.

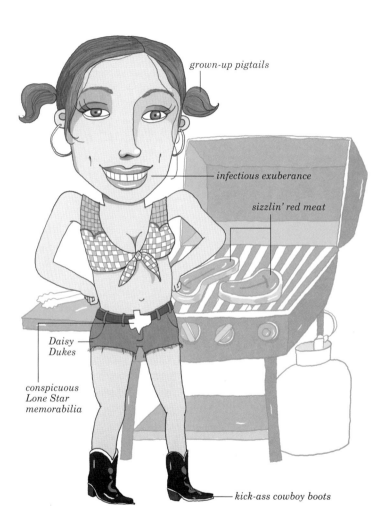

grown-up pigtails

infectious exuberance

sizzlin' red meat

Daisy Dukes

conspicuous Lone Star memorabilia

kick-ass cowboy boots

the obsessively optimistic friend

HABITAT: Pinkberry, sample sales, Pilates

IDENTIFYING CHARACTERISTICS: Pearls, translucent white teeth, John Mayer CD

PRO: Reintroduces you to Crystal Light and impressionism

CON: Provides false sense of security

CATCHPHRASE: "No problem!"

The identifying phraseology of the Obsessively Optimistic Friend is "no problem." She has immaculate hair and skin to go along with her immaculate driving record. Her apartment boasts a calming color palette she will inevitably describe as "café au lait and robin's egg blue." She watches Lifetime without irony and considers the second Gin and Tonic a wild night out. She can put a peppy spin on anything. Going through a breakup? He's miserable right now, and you're fabulous! The OOF never gains weight and doesn't believe in dieting. She just eats right! She is your cheerleader, career counselor, and the one friend your mother continually asks about. But it's hard to take her seriously sometimes, what with the Burberry headbands and all. You may want to scream, "There's a war on, for Christ's sake! Ethnic cleansing in Darfur! Global warming!" But don't expect much other than, "Ew, depressing! Did you see *Dancing with the Stars*?"

WHAT TO DO

Bolster your friendship with periodic girls' nights and Daily Candy Alerts, and try not to feel inadequate.

the retail therapy friend

HABITAT: Prowling the sales rack

IDENTIFYING CHARACTERISTICS: Big Brown Bag, this season's heels, bulging, receipt-filled wallet

PRO: Free personal stylist

CON: Nonreturnable impulse buys

CATCHPHRASE: "Just try it on!"

Shopping with the Retail Therapy Friend can be both instructive ("Beware the belted top") and emboldening ("Wide-leg pant? Yes you can!"). The RTF has boundless energy, a keen eye, and sharply honed tactics for deflecting bitchy sales girls. She'll brush off their commission-hungry attempts at personal service and jettison an armload of prized pieces over the dressing-room door. She ignores your protests that it's too tight or too short, assuring you that "it can never be too tight or too short!" Until you shimmy out and she admits, "Maybe it can." But fear not, the RTF will always blame bad tailoring or wretched dressing-room lighting for any unflattering ensembles, never your physique. When you finally emerge in something that fits, she'll gasp with unbridled delight and march you to the cash register before you can change your mind. She's also good at buying you a few drinks afterward and assuring you that you have made not just a wise purchase, but the Greatest Purchase of All Time.

WHAT TO DO

Admit you are powerless over retail and hold on to this friend as you would a brand-new Balenciaga bag.

the cute tech geek friend

HABITAT: Chat room, CES, Genius Bar, 4G iPhone

IDENTIFYING CHARACTERISTICS: Glasses, high-tops, power cords

PRO: Fixes your ailing laptop

CON: Makes you feel helpless and retarded

CATCHPHRASE: "You backed everything up, right?"

If the Cute Tech Geek Friend works at your company, she's in demand: Every male employee quietly requests "the IT girl" to help them with their (usually fictional) computer problems, and they all stare at her longingly as she toggles around and sighs at their incompetence. She tends to be a little twitchy and distracted when not interfacing with an operating system, and when around other IT professionals she'll talk for hours about obscure coding issues and laugh with genuine disdain at the dorkiness of Vista. She can be ruthless in her tech snobbery—she once dumped a guy for having a Dell. It can be a bummer when you proudly brandish your fancy new laptop or gadget and she sighs, saying, "I'm going to wait for the beta version" and then explains, in detail, why your $2,800 purchase is going to be obsolete in two months. But she's a great friend to have when your term paper or job presentation goes 404 or, most crucially, when you've drunk e-mailed an ex.

WHAT TO DO

Always back up this friendship!

geeky IT girl glasses

tech-snob smirk

Nerdcore buttons

spare power cord

dorky-cool high-tops

the wingman friend

HABITAT: Intimidating parties, road trip vacations, the clinic

IDENTIFYING CHARACTERISTICS: Similar style as yours, great laugh, social stamina

PRO: Is your best pal for life

CON: Are you codependent?

CATCHPHRASE: "Don't look. He's looking over here."

The Wingman Friend is the one you choose to accompany you everywhere. Trolling for guys, attending showers, cooking parties (and other painful girls-only events), braving a Saturday at IKEA, attending concerts by marginal bands, hanging out with you all night while your boyfriend is at a bachelor party—she's there. She can always be counted on in any given situation, laughs at your jokes, shares your fashion sense, and gives you honest assessments of your faults and unequivocal accolades for your strengths. You actually do not know what you would do without her. Guys are great and all, but most of them have a rather basic, bovine understanding of the terrors and dizzying heights of ladyhood, whereas your Wingman Friend gets it, on all possible levels, and you're damn lucky to have her.

WHAT TO DO

Never ditch her for a guy.

the gay friend

HABITAT: Paul Smith, kitschy-fun piano bar, Bliss Spa

IDENTIFYING CHARACTERISTICS: Toned abs, killer shoes, "it" belt

PRO: Fantastic fashion advice, is brutally honest, cares about Britney

CON: Sometimes you feel like you're a mutual cliché

CATCHPHRASE: "Sweetheart, let's get you a Lillet."

Sometimes you want to have girl talk without dealing with a girl, and there's no better companion than the Gay Friend. He flatters, he shops, he has impeccable taste, and he tells it like it is. The Gay Friend likes to talk about relationships—from one-night stands to fiancés, it doesn't matter—which is great because you get a male perspective filtered through a rose-tinted lens of gayness. The Gay Friend is also, as has been chronicled in innumerable chick-flick films and sitcoms, an impeccable date for weddings and other obligatory events. Not only will he look sharper, be wittier, and smell better than 99 percent of the male population, he won't make you dance to "Brick House." Instead he will elect to sit with you at the table, knocking back champagne and engaging in a running commentary on various fashion violations and tragic couplings at said event.

WHAT TO DO

Never, ever introduce him as "my gay husband" or "my main gay," or refer to yourself as a "fag hag." That demeans you both.

threat level blue
The Low-Risk Friend

The Threat Level Blue Friend is what you might call a
B list or second-tier friend. You can usually count on her
for companionship, support, or a sudden wine-mergency,
and she rarely shows signs of fakery, bitchery, or random
frostiness. Best in a group setting, she should be included
on party guest lists and invited to significant birthday
celebrations, or be prepared for months,
even years, of awkwardness.

the everything
to everyone friend

HABITAT: Varies wildly

IDENTIFYING CHARACTERISTICS: None

PRO: You have so much in common!

CON: You have no idea who she is

CATCHPHRASE: "I don't care. What do *you* want to do?"

The Everything to Everyone Friend is less a social chameleon than a shape-shifter. One night she's head banging at a Norwegian death metal show, the next she's earnestly discussing welfare reform over responsibly farmed green tea. Her mannerisms, accessories, and speech patterns alter themselves based on her immediate company. She always seems to understand exactly where you're coming from, but you'll often catch her in a moment of flushed inattention that indicates she's not actually all that invested in the conversation. You say something to the effect of "So they think it's malignant." And she'll reply, "That's awesome!" Generally a safe harbor, the Everything to Everyone Friend can still be exasperating. You may, over time, come to view her as shallow, all façade, merely mirroring her contemporaries, a parakeet in Jimmy Choos. But be warned: She's by nature a people pleaser, so if you act annoyed she will pick up on it immediately and begin to subtly flatter her way back into your good graces.

WHAT TO DO

Keep her around. Ditching her would be like ditching your shadow—unnecessary and impossible.

the suddenly single friend

HABITAT: Any bar, any time

IDENTIFYING CHARACTERISTICS: Embroidered tank, frenzied expression, outdated accessories

PRO: Parties again!

CON: Then gets sad

CATCHPHRASE: "I'm so movin' on / yeah yeah!"

The Suddenly Single Friend is typically a "relationship girl," one of the charmed few who manages to effortlessly breeze from one long-term gig to another. But things fall apart, and one day she finds herself sans-BF, with weeks and weekends stretching out before her, stripped of the cozy reliability of movie nights, shared bottles of Pinot, semi-strenuous hikes, and other sweetly mundane relationship activities. Faced with newfound freedom, she hibernates for two weeks, sheds some misery weight, pulls her suggestive clothes to the forefront of her closet, and calls you, saying she wants to go out. Tonight! She's putting Jeff and his BS behind her. She is OVER IT. For real! Wooooo! As a Suddenly Single girl, she has something to prove: that she is still hot, desirable, and attractive post-breakup. You may be glad to have your friend back, but keep in mind that her current state of social enthusiasm may be short-lived. Odds are she'll get back together with Jeff, or go full-throttle into a rebound with someone who looks suspiciously like Jeff.

WHAT TO DO

Ride the wave of her social momentum while it lasts, and never let her call Jeff from the bar.

the "I went to Nepal and it totally changed my perspective" friend

HABITAT: Drum circle, sustainable architecture lecture, noodle house

IDENTIFYING CHARACTERISTICS: Steady gaze, walking boots, sacred objects

PRO: Shares her dahl-bat recipe

CON: Won't shut up about Nepal

CATCHPHRASE: "That line of thinking is positively Maoist."

She used to be a fun girl: She liked shopping and fancy steakhouses and wasn't ashamed to profess a crush on a network reality-show cast member. She had undisguised scorn for fakers, prudes, teetotalers, and guys who wore man-sandals. Then she went to Nepal, and the person who returned bore no resemblance to the girl you used to call your friend. Eschewing smoking and gossiping for the milder pleasures of sipping organic herbal tea and chanting, she took up with a strange group of pierced nomads. "This is Ananda," she'll say. "But we all call her Snow Leopard." As you're complaining about your boring job or listless boyfriend, she'll respond with, "The greatest medicine is the emptiness of everything." You may be tempted to view her transformation as a personal affront, but keep in mind there is much to be gained by the influence of your new, clear-minded, searcher friend. Including, but not limited to, hot activist boys.

WHAT TO DO

Stick with her. Perhaps you, too, can make a difference!

steady, visionary gaze

organic herbal tea

sacred objects from Nepalese holy man

decorative beadwork

Himalayan walking boots

the questionable sexuality friend

HABITAT: Softball game, after-hours girl club, over at her boyfriend's

IDENTIFYING CHARACTERISTICS: Shorts, piercings, impeccably styled hair

PRO: Loves everyone!

CON: *Everyone.*

CATCHPHRASE: "Margaret Cho cracks my sh-t up!"

Is she or isn't she? Questionable Sexuality Friend is cagey about her sex life. In these enlightened times it shouldn't be an issue, really, but it can still confound you when you spend all night watching her flirt with hot Australian businessmen, then later she sends you a text that says, "You are sexy." Usually you laugh it off and chalk it up to one too many vodka-crans, but you just wish she'd be slightly less mysterious about which team she's playing for. Her reluctance to reveal the true nature of her sexuality seems like evidence of your own rigidity, and you want her to know that you're open-minded! You kissed a girl once, in college! You love *Ellen*! Don't say any of this, though, as it will only emphasize your sheltered suburban upbringing, cause her to be even more evasive, and possibly make you the subject of ridicule among her cool gay friends.

WHAT TO DO

Wait until she (finally) announces that she "needs to talk to you about something." Then be real supportive.

the bad-taste-in-music friend

HABITAT: Adult Contemporary section, Lilith Fair reunion show, Jimmy Buffet concert

IDENTIFYING CHARACTERISTICS: Banana Republic sweater, benign jeans, ZUNE player

PRO: Isn't a snob

CON: Too . . . much . . . James . . . Taylor!

CATCHPRHASE: "I love that song!" (at any indoor or outdoor shopping plaza) or "This music is weird!" (anywhere else)

She may have excellent taste in food, wine, literature, and men, but for some reason she never quite got around to developing taste in music. Perhaps she never had a disgusted older brother around to tear down her Backstreet Boys poster and blast the Ramones. She owns roughly seven CDs and a dated MP3 player that dutifully shuffles Ruben Studdard, Sting, James Taylor, Jack Johnson, Seal, the soundtrack to an unspecified Sandra Bullock movie, Maroon 5, and either Frank Sinatra or Bing Crosby. She may announce that she's created a party mix, giving you momentary hope, until you discover that it's the exact same handful of bands, with one "rap" song by one or all of the Black Eyed Peas. Maybe if she dates a disparaging rock snob, things will change, but until then, strap in for another round of "Starry Eyed Surprise."

WHAT TO DO

It is no use trying to introduce BTIMF to new styles of music. Just grin and bear it—and avoid long road trips.

the perpetually-trying-to-lose-ten-pounds friend

HABITAT: Jamba Juice, Crunch Gym, Ben & Jerry's

IDENTIFYING CHARACTERISTICS: Empire waists, billowy tops, mod dresses

PRO: Spurs you to greater heights of dieting resolve

CON: Is never going to lose ten pounds

CATCHPHRASE: "I just need to lose ten pounds."

The Perpetually-Trying-to-Lose-Ten-Pounds Friend doesn't have a major self-image problem, and she certainly isn't overweight. For some reason she has decided that the key to happiness is fitting into her size 4 jeans (the mythical pair that she had no problem with before she went to college and pigged out on Crusty's™ Pizza Stix every night . . . or when she and Mike broke up and she didn't eat because she was just too sad. Anyway.). Now, after a few years of nightly happy hours and lackadaisical gym attendance, she finds it impossible to meet her weight goal. Sometimes she's merely fishing for reassurance ("Please, you look amazing"), other times just solidarity ("Oh my god, me too! I had another cookie dough incident last night"), but you both know that barring some sort of debilitating stomach virus, traumatic breakup, or Peace Corps stint, her ardent wish will never be fulfilled.

WHAT TO DO

Be supportive of her goal, but bear in mind, if she does manage to lose ten pounds, you'll have nothing to talk about.

relentlessly
self-critical gaze

pseudo-nutritious
fruit drink

empire-waist
dress

the staggeringly successful friend

HABITAT: Racquet club, co-op board meeting, Neiman Marcus

IDENTIFYING CHARACTERISTICS: Crisp, tailored suits; breezy air of unconcern

PRO: Gives you a ride in her 7-Series

CON: Reminding you how much you hate the bus

CATCHPHRASE: "Greetings from Hotel Du Cap!"

You grew up in similar comfortable middle-class homes and went to similar colleges. But once you graduated, the roads diverged, and you took the path less traveled by, while she took the one that ends in spa weeks in Pueblo Tulum. Far from downplaying her newfound fortune (à la the calmly entitled Preppy Friend), the Staggeringly Successful Friend is delighted with her success and likes to talk about it. Try not to be confounded or jealous; remind yourself that some people are born with the drive to Make It to the Top, while others drift around from one vague career choice to one ill-fated stab at law school after another until finally admitting that they don't have a calling in life, or if they do, it's a very quiet one. No biggie! It's fun to visit her home (or homes), which have a crisp, grown-up feeling, quality deli meats, plush linens, and rich, blackcurrant-y cabernets. But it only makes it more difficult to head back to your IKEA couch and annoying roommates.

WHAT TO DO

Be there for her if the market crashes, and suggest that this holiday season you do "no gifts" in lieu of last year's Cartier-bracelet-vs.-Bath-&-Body-Works debacle.

the "I saw on Oprah" friend

HABITAT: Couch, 4 P.M.

IDENTIFYING CHARACTERISTICS: Camel tones, LIVESTRONG bracelet

PRO: So empathetic! So motivational!

CON: Has no opinion other than Oprah's

CATCHPHRASE: "Celebrate and honor *you*!"

The "I Saw on *Oprah*" Friend's devotion to Oprah is evangelical. What Oprah says goes, whether it's a lean meat diet, a juice diet, or no dieting at all because you should accept yourself as the beautiful woman you are! What Oprah recommends, this friend adopts, reading *Love in the Time of Cholera* while rolling out Outrageous Oreo Crunch brownies and painting her cabinetry navy. When Oprah's dog died, the "I saw on *Oprah*" Friend shed very real tears. It's understandable: Oprah is a cultural arbiter, an undeniably charismatic philanthropist, and a strong supporter of the written word (hi, Oprah!). The ISOO is a good listener, but tends to relate everything to *Oprah*, which can get conversationally dicey, especially if today's episode is about AIDS in West Virginia. But it's worthwhile to have someone in your life who is all about empowerment, even if you do wonder how someone so personally motivated manages to watch so much TV in the middle of the day.

WHAT TO DO

Enjoy her optimism and candor, and be sure to occasionally remind her that she isn't actually friends with Oprah.

the sex advice friend

HABITAT: Erotica section of bookstore, Kiki de Montparnasse, upscale burlesque club

IDENTIFYING CHARACTERISTICS: Cat's-eye reading glasses, conservative suit, fishnets

PRO: Puts it out there

CON: Makes you feel prudish and repressed

CATCHPHRASE: "Try this . . ."

Every girl has one friend who dishes the sex advice with cool authority. She's not really perverse or into obscure and/or scary stuff; she's just somehow seen it all, done it all, and doesn't mind talking about it all. If you have an embarrassing question ("So then he said he wanted to . . . do you think I should?"), she'll give not just good advice, but an entire philosophy. Her discretion is legendary—you know she's not going to be spreading the word that you dressed up like a sexy stewardess and it backfired. She'll talk you through vibrators, threeways, odd fetishes, strip clubs, sex clubs, lube choices, roommate orgies, and "how to give a killer BJ." She has a laundry list of suitors past, present, and sporadic but tends not to settle down, which is a good thing, because once Sex Advice Friend gets a steady boyfriend or husband, suddenly she becomes less saucy and salacious and more imbued with "enjoy it while you can" melancholy.

WHAT TO DO

Hold on to this scandalous friend. You'll get all of your intimate questions answered—without an embarrassing Google history!

sexy librarian up-do

cat's-eye reading glasses

Kiki de Montparnasse lingerie

conservative suit

sex toys

fishnets

the design-y friend

HABITAT: MUJI, Apple Store, *Dwell* magazine party, Boffi showroom

IDENTIFYING CHARACTERISTICS: Scandinavian print dress, black framed glasses

PRO: Smart, caustic, redesigns your Evite for you

CON: Mocks your Jennifer Convertibles coffee table

CATCHPHRASE: "If it's not Bulthaup, you're just really wasting your time."

The Design-y Friend was into design way before it got trendy. She was hunting down Hans Wegner chairs long before they graced the glossy pages of mainstream shelter magazines. She cares deeply about the manufactured world, and desperately wishes things could be more Finnish. Her home is a showroom, and she requests that you refer to her furniture as "pieces." She can discuss at length the sociopolitical impact of an ottoman, and although wry and sophisticated, she can be kind of a humorless windbag at times. You care about the Italian textile revolution of the 1960s, you really do, but you also care about other things, like another drink, which she may be slow to pour because she feels the need to discuss her new Moss champagne flutes and how their clean, minimalist approach is a bracing affront to the current culture of quasi-regency adornment, which she thinks, frankly, is a step back. Enough shoptalk, sister, and hurry with the sparkly stuff!

WHAT TO DO

Say you're "getting into design" yourself and heading to IKEA for inspiration. Watch her quietly fume.

the empowered woman friend

HABITAT: Girls' night, wine bar, Races for the Cure

IDENTIFYING CHARACTERISTICS: Tunics, turquoise jewelry, the carefree countenance of the non-guy-obsessed

PRO: Is in touch with her feminine side

CON: So . . . much . . . estrogen!

CATCHPHRASE: "Chicks rule!"

The Empowered Woman Friend isn't a hard-line feminist. She's not even very political. For her, being a woman, and proud of it, is a lifestyle, and one that provides a great source of satisfaction, social solidarity, and free T-shirts. If there's a woman-related cause, she's there, walking, running, supporting, and bidding on art of questionable merit. She ventures to South America with women's travel collectives, starts up "women and wine" groups, heads women-in-business organizations, and is generally very proactive and inspiring, even if she is exhausting and sort of intense. On that note, while the Empowered Woman Friend is a priceless ally if you suspect you're being harassed at work, she might not be the best person to take for a couple of drinks at the Regal Beagle. There's no one guys find scarier than an Empowered Woman.

WHAT TO DO

Join her on a power walk on Susan B. Anthony Day.
Sisterhood, unite!

the jam band friend

HABITAT: Phish reunion tour, drum circle, The Playa

IDENTIFYING CHARACTERISTICS: Long skirt, single cornrow, pierced eyebrows

PRO: Fun and swirly!

CON: Endless guitar noodling

CATCHPHRASE: "You just had to be there."

When Jerry Garcia died, he left a serious void in the psychedelic/ good vibes/let's-dress-like-a-deranged-court-jester-and-hallucinate-in-public community. But fortunately (for some), a new crop of popular, if musically tepid, jam bands rose from the spent hash pipes of the Dead's following, and Jam Band Friend was on board! Just as the Dead created a sense of peace and community, so, in a limited sense, do they. The venues might be smaller and the guitar solos might be interminable, but never underestimate what a handful of mushrooms washed down with a frosty mug of home-brewed beer will do for one's appreciation of a musical genre. Jam Band Friend will often disappear for months at a time, touring with the band, lighting joss sticks, indulging in various altered states of consciousness. You'll hear from her infrequently, save for strange missives posted on her blog, erratically punctuated and usually drifting off into what you sincerely hope are song lyrics.

WHAT TO DO

Keep on truckin' with this friend! But bring earplugs.

altered state
of consciousness

slightly infected
pierced eyebrow

endless guitar
noodling

single cornrow

trash-picked
beanbag chair

long swirly skirt

the terminal exaggerator friend

HABITAT: IN JAIL! (almost) IN THE HOSPITAL! (sort of) SITTING NEXT TO GEORGE CLOONEY! (practically)

IDENTIFYING CHARACTERISTICS: Blinks a lot

PRO: Tells amazing anecdotes

CON: You're pretty sure none of them actually happened

CATCHPHRASE: "You'll never believe it . . ." (You never do)

The Terminal Exaggerator tells it like it ain't. She's not maliciously deceitful and doesn't usually outright lie, she just has an overactive imagination mixed with an entertainer's need to polish the material a bit. In her eyes, an incident becomes a predicament. A mishap becomes a disaster. And so on, and so on, until her free scoop of gelato turns into a hilarious ten-minute tale of true love, betrayal, and redemption. As such, you have to take everything she says with a grain of salt. It doesn't help to call her out ("Was it really Dolly Parton who loaned you a tampon in the bathroom at Caesars?"), because she'll just concoct a more elaborate secondary exaggeration, which could take all night. You can usually tell when a story goes from sort of true to absolutely implausible by a certain telltale pause and gleam in her eye as she continues: "And then . . . the pilot said the plane was out of fuel . . . so we had to fly backward!" Uh-huh.

WHAT TO DO

Enjoy her alternate reality but never ask her to serve as a character reference.

the crude friend

HABITAT: Movie theaters, lingerie departments, any public place

IDENTIFYING CHARACTERISTICS: Pretty, gregarious, always chewing gum

PRO: Isn't held back by Puritan hang-ups

CON: You wish she'd keep her voice down

CATCHPHRASE: "Suck my left tit!"

The Crude Friend has no conversational filter whatsoever. Bawdy and unrestrained, she comes out with shocking and admittedly pretty creative riffs on common expletives and derogatory jargon. She tends to have a booming, gravelly voice that seriously carries. She tones it down around guys and parents, usually, but with other, more timid friends things can get dicey. Watch your Aggressively Christian Friend blanch as she greets you with a hearty, "What's up, biznatch?" and then relates that she had an awesome time in New Orleans at what she refers to as "JizzFest." If you find yourself in an employment situation with the Crude Friend, do not sit next to her in meetings, as her sketchpad will become a catalyst for uncontrollable hilarity . . . and possible lawsuits.

WHAT TO DO

Brace yourself and relish her ribald company. JizzFest? That's funny!

the lightweight friend

HABITAT: Callin' it a night

IDENTIFYING CHARACTERISTICS: The glazed, euphoric, slightly manic look of the easily buzzed

PRO: Will buy rounds even though she can't drink them

CON: It's like taking candy from a drunken baby

CATCHPHRASE: "Whoops!"

The Lightweight Friend can handle exactly 1.5 alcoholic beverages. The effect of said beverages tends to take effect after the second or third sip. It could be something as innocuous as a light pilsner or a white wine spritzer, but no matter—she'll still get flushed, giggly, and hiccup-y, and signal to the bartender for a Diet Coke. She might have one of those sensitivity-to-booze genes that affect some people or just be really skinny. On her 21st birthday, she may have gone balls-out and had three drinks, but it wasn't pretty. The strange thing is, Lightweight Friend tends to go through the whole inebriation spiral, only faster. In the span of an hour she'll go from sober to buzzed to drunk to wasted, and often reach the presentiment of a hangover before you've even finished your first Manhattan. The Lightweight is generally a fun and benign presence, not to mention a cheap date. Plus, when was the last time you heard someone order a Zima?

WHAT TO DO

Marvel at her metabolism, but never take her to Vegas or Mexico.

the terminally laid-back friend

HABITAT: Sleeping in, hanging out, chilling

IDENTIFYING CHARACTERISTICS: Leggings, Havaianas, imprint from sofa cushions on face

PRO: So unhurried and cool

CON: And catatonic

CATCHPHRASE: "Take it easy."

The Terminally Laid-Back Friend has no get-up-and-go. Unless there is an obligatory social occasion, especially cute boy, or free cocktail involved, she isn't leaving the house. She often breaks her own personal records for sleeping in (the latest was 6 P.M.) and can remain motionless, like a swamp alligator, for hours on end, watching the worst television ever conceived by a VH1 programming director. You may call and suggest a nice walk in the park or movie, only to be greeted with a pause, and then, "I have a lot of things to get done today," over the suspicious droning of *America's Next Top Model*. If you manage to get her out into the world, she seems to be on a ten-second delay, laughing at jokes you made a few moments ago and blinking uncomfortably in the sunlight. Eventually she'll suggest the two of you head back to her place and "chill for a bit." Tyra, here you come.

WHAT TO DO

Enjoy her mellow personality but consider chipping in for an espresso machine, NordicTrack, or amphetamine prescription for her next birthday.

threat level yellow
The Moderate-Risk Friend

A Threat Level Yellow Friend tends to be an obligatory friend—someone you've befriended due to proximity or circumstance, not necessarily by choice. She isn't mean or spiteful, but neither is she particularly relatable or fun. She's just sort of . . . there. As you'll see, this can be either a good or a profoundly irritating thing.

the outdoorsy friend

HABITAT: North Face outlets, headlands of any kind, Boulder, CO

IDENTIFYING CHARACTERISTICS: Performance wear, packet of muesli, T-shirt layered over long-sleeved T-shirt

PRO: Occasionally gets you off the couch

CON: Doesn't understand that napping is a legitimate pursuit

CATCHPHRASE: "It's beautiful out! Let's go do something!"

On any weekend day, the Outdoorsy Friend must hike, climb, mountain-bike, windsurf, or rappel. Staying inside on a sunny Saturday is not mere laziness, it's a moral failing, and she's good about making you feel bad about it. She considers a fanny pack a functional accessory and drives a car with state-of-the-art racks attached. These racks, along with her ever-present North Face fleece, label her an Outdoorsy Person, meant to attract fellow seekers of surf, sun, and mesh shorts. She will meet many Outdoorsy Guys this way, and they're all tan, half-bearded, and boring. When you manage to coax her out for a cocktail, she seems itchy and uncomfortable in clothes that aren't designed to breathe and trap heat at the same time. She'll pull at her collar, and gaze down longingly at her carabineer keychain, announcing after an hour that she must go, since she has a 15-mile vertical hike at seven and "wants to be pumped." You finish her drink.

WHAT TO DO

Perhaps one day her spirit of the wild will rub off on you, but until then feel free to screen her calls on weekends.

hand-whittled
walking stick

T-shirt layered over
long-sleeved T-shirt

fully functional
fanny pack

carabiner
keychain

rock-solid calves

the suburban friend

HABITAT: Jazzercise, Safeway parking lot, Ace Hardware

IDENTIFYING CHARACTERISTICS: Nike power-walking gear, sub-par highlights, Tiffany key ring

PRO: Has a pool

CON: Has turned into her mom

CATCHPHRASE: "I just love the peace and quiet!"

For some, getting out of the suburbs is a defining moment. At a young, surly age, they reject these cozy pockets of Spanish tile and Olive Gardens as the epitome of American mediocrity and spiritual dissipation. Others love it! Plenty of parking, tree-lined streets, good schools—what's not to love? And *hello*, the Olive Garden is *good*! Bottomless breadsticks, yo! Lack of diversity, megaplexes that consider a Will Smith movie edgy, and homogeneous architecture are all taken in stride. When Suburban Friend visits a city, she tackles it like a tourist and prefers to go to familiar establishments, like Sonic Burger or sports bars. You may get jealous of her four-bedroom home, private backyard, and kitchen appliances, but you've got to figure that when Friday night rolls around and the options are Pizza Poppers at T.G.I. Friday's or Taco Sliders at El Torito, it's got to get a little old. And yet it never does.

WHAT TO DO

Head to the suburbs for the pool parties, but always have an exit strategy, such as: "I'm on my way to the airport."

the preppy friend

HABITAT: JG Mellon, Lily Pulitzer, the Cape

IDENTIFYING CHARACTERISTICS: Ribbon belt embroidered with wee spouting whales

PRO: Is crisp, clean, and grew-up-with-ponies confident

CON: Ruthless snob

CATCHPHRASE: "Wheels up at 2 P.M.!"

The Preppy Friend's charms are like a spring breeze—sometimes a cool caress, other times frigid and infuriating. She is not like the well-documented '80s preppies, who were frankly clannish and overtly materialistic; instead she keeps her swank upbringing under wraps, save for a few throwback habits. She wears Lacoste, and not in a funky-retro way. She irons sheets. She lunches. She summers. She wears pearls and has whopping diamond earrings from Dad. She believes in having a career and developing her creative side, so she goes to fashion school or becomes a jewelry maker/florist/freelance event planner before settling down and supporting charitable causes. She has a sailboat and a husband with a full head of golden-retriever-blond hair and a live-in maid whom she refers to as a personal assistant. She also might have an actual personal assistant. You like her because she treats you like an equal, and resent her because you have the sneaking suspicion that you're not.

WHAT TO DO

Even if you feel like Gilligan to her captain, it's still fun to be on the boat.

the new mom friend

HABITAT: Babies 'R' Us, Pottery Barn Kids, Paranoid New Mom's Support Group

IDENTIFYING CHARACTERISTICS: Odd combination of The Glow and The Postpartum Depresssh

PRO: Has brought new life into the world

CON: Uses the term "engorged" in casual conversation

CATCHPHRASE: "Do you want to hold him/her?"

The New Mom Friend has just been through an awe-inspiring experience. You feel the Awe, but you also feel an emotion akin to blind panic the second you come into the baby's room. Your first thought is likely to be, "Please don't ask me to hold the baby." But she does. You try to affect a maternal pose but eventually the little one starts to cry or cough or barf, and you return it to its rightful owner, to the relief of all. Part of you senses that she's dying to talk about anything other than her Diaper Genie, and that your gifts of onesies and stork-bedecked blankets would be so much better if they were Fekkai products and gin. But the little guy or girl in the room sucks all the energy away like a tiny bald vortex. New Mom Friend may try to keep up appearances, but she's a different person now, a mom. The gulf between you seems significant, and you feel like you're letting your uterus down.

WHAT TO DO

Give her time. Once she's done breastfeeding, you can totally party again!

the sanctimonious activist friend

HABITAT: Obscure collectives, agit-prop meetings, Good Earth Grocery

IDENTIFYING CHARACTERISTICS: Earth-toned head scarf, Tom's of Maine deodorant, petitions

PRO: Is noble, cares fiercely

CON: Thinks you're materialistic, vain, and petty. Is probably right.

CATCHPHRASE: "The depth of today's apathy makes me sick."

The Sanctimonious Activist has a cause. It could be something as big and accessible as The Environment or something as specific and confusing as labor rights in Zhejiang. You're likely to never quite understand the issue, and although you try to be supportive by attending a potluck or two, your heart isn't in it. She most likely picked up the activist bug in college, where she sat outside the student center behind a card table with an obscure acronym painted on it, yelling into a bullhorn while a coterie of short, scruffy, semi-cute liberal guys raised their fists in righteous assent. She went or is going to a graduate program in Peace and Conflict Studies. She owns more that one clipboard. You won't be able to discuss *The Hills* or how you can't believe your hairstylist gave you bangs, but in her fierce company your worldview might broaden! You might learn to empathize and feel the plight of those less fortunate! And don't worry, the bangs will grow in.

WHAT TO DO

Stick around. Who knows, you might feel passionate-by-proxy!

the weird interests friend

HABITAT: Comic-Con, Renaissance faire, S&M party

IDENTIFYING CHARACTERISTICS: Jester hat, wench bustier, oversized chicken leg, anime T-shirt

PRO: Has a real community and tight-knit group of friends

CON: They scare you

CATCHPHRASE: "Forsooth, my liege, this mead flows free!"

Weird Interests Friend transcends mere hobbyist or enthusiast status. She's not a fan, but a *fanatic* about something, and it usually involves the past, the imagined future, chalices, or cross-stitched leather pants. She may seem relaxed and cool in your daily interactions, and she's not a shut-in or obsessive, but once you get her going on the subject of her affection you may pray for one of those Monty Burns–style trapdoor buttons. Her fervor is genuine, but puzzling. It's tough to remember the varying degrees of fiefdom, and let's face it: Everyone has their own strange desires and hidden obsessions, but the manifestation of one's passion in fictional worlds has a hint of, oh, let's just say it, nerdiness that puts her perilously close to uncool. That said, if you can keep the subject matter neutral and manage to deflect her pleas for you to join Second Life, she is probably a kind (and creative!) pal.

WHAT TO DO

Remain friendly, but never oversolicitous.
And don't peek in her closet.

trusty jousting steed

jester hat

Henry VIII chicken leg

wench costume

anachronistic footwear

the kicky DIY friend

HABITAT: The Yarn Barn, Williamsburg Renegade Craft Festival, BYO parties

IDENTIFYING CHARACTERISTICS: Reupholstered vintage buttons, hand-knitted scarf, hummingbird babydoll dress

PRO: Resourceful

CON: Smug

CATCHPHRASE: "Are you going to throw that away?"

If it were the '90s, she would have been your Thrift Store Friend. But the tides have turned, and now DIY is the preferred fashion outlet for cute, socially conscious girls. She and her group of crafty pals wear their anti-materialism on their sleeves. They're against the Man, but not in an aggressive anarchist way—in a let's-make-a-bunch-of-felt-eyeballs way. Her interests also lie in indie music, indie boys, felt, American Spirits, sangria, and making her own grainy, unintelligible Super-8 films. She's cool, and you wish you had her passion and creativity, but something about her irks you. You know her commitment to the handmade is both hip and environmentally responsible, but sometimes she's just a *lit*-tle too pleased with her handiwork—and herself. You end up feeling cloddish because you don't share her view that crochet is a subversive activity, and unduly wasteful for purchasing a pair of shoes instead of cobbling them yourself.

WHAT TO DO

Maintain a lo-effort friendship. Who knows, some day you might want to make an armoire out of Orange Crush bottle caps. Someday.

the Blabby
McBlabberton friend

HABITAT: Coffee shops, airplanes, elevators, department stores, moving sidewalks, funeral homes, yachts, long drives, office parties, drug stores . . .

IDENTIFYING CHARACTERISTICS: Newfangled Bluetooth headset, constant yapping

PRO: Doesn't spare you the details

CON: Doesn't spare anyone else the details, either

CATCHPHRASE: "Don't repeat this."

Here's how to tell if you've got a Blabby McBlabberton Friend on your hands: Tell her you've got a secret—something so deep, so dark, that she must swear never to reveal it to a soul. Watch her nod solemnly and promise. Then make something up. Whatever fictional personal detail you reveal will be all over town, and possibly the Internet, not within hours, but minutes. Your fling with Brett Favre, your conversion to Scientology, your secret life as a dominatrix—it's all on public record. Blabby is an eloquent and loquacious gossip, unable to retain information without sharing it. It's clear she just wants attention—and nothing gets attention like a juicy bit of scandal. If you can train yourself not to reveal anything personal, you'll likely be clued in on the very freshest dispatches from your mutual social world. But tread carefully, since Blabby is also quite good at making stuff up as well.

WHAT TO DO

Keep things close to the vest and never over-imbibe in her presence.

the secret shame friend

HABITAT: The ladies' room

IDENTIFYING CHARACTERISTICS: Long sleeves, thin frame, Smiths CD, excuses

PROS: Makes you feel like you have it together

CONS: Worries you to death

CATCHPHRASE: Choked-back sobs

Is it an eating disorder? A cutting problem? A pervy uncle? Something's going on with her, but whatever it is, she isn't telling. The Secret Shame Friend is a master of deception, a Svengali of casual lies. Discussing the latest *Dateline* "Drugs in the Heartland" exposé, she may scoff, "Meth is so 2005," before borrowing $50 and disappearing for two days. Or she'll look accusingly at the nineteen-year-old intern and whisper, "Hello, bulimic," before polishing off two pints of mint chip ice cream and slipping off to the handicapped stall. These incidents aside, the Secret Shame Friend is so adept at concealing that sometimes you're not even sure if there is a problem or if you just watch too much *Dr. Phil*. So you're stuck in limbo—to frankly broach the subject would obliterate the friendship; to remain silent puts you in that unfortunate category of "enabler." Although she is likely a smart, complex, and darkly humorous companion, you never know whether to lighten up or schedule an intervention.

WHAT TO DO

Try to get her to "seek help." It's awkward, but necessary.
Thanks, Dr. Phil.

the always-in-love friend

HABITAT: Where the boys are

IDENTIFYING CHARACTERISTICS: Glittering eyes, extra layer of perfume, air of exhilaration

PRO: Is always in love, thus making you believe in love

CON: Gets dumped a lot, making you believe there is no such thing as love

CATCHPHRASE: "This is The One."

The Always-in-Love Friend is convinced that she's found the man of her dreams roughly three times a month. Her relationships are frequent but short-lived, especially once she tells him he's The One. Guys don't really like that. But during that first flush of infatuation, the Always-in-Love Friend will smile dreamily as she describes how they met (it's always an adorable coincidence: He took her latte by mistake, hee!), and any subsequent discourse with her will be punctured with the bleeps of her cell phone as he texts or e-mails and she responds, euphorically. This uninhibited bliss quickly mutates into panic and insecurity as his texts grow fewer and fewer. Then you're AIL friend will need reassurance—in this case quite easy to provide—that there are other fish in the sea. And the next fish will be The One!

WHAT TO DO

Enjoy the madcap romantic comedy that is her life and keep (fake) smilin'!

the magic sparkle pegasus powder friend

HABITAT: Gross club bathroom stall, ATM, Colombia

IDENTIFYING CHARACTERISTICS: Unblinking, teeth-grinding, chatty

PRO: Is so interested in everything you have to say

CON: Isn't actually listening

CATCHPHRASE: "This is great. I feel awesome!"

The Magic Sparkle Pegasus Powder Friend will be *right* back. She's just going to run to the bathroom for a sec! Repeat. A recreational party-gal, the MSPPF is discreet, well-off, and usually discovered her vice later in life, when alcohol got boring and pot made her sleepy and hungry. If you happen to go to dinner with the MSPP Friend, she's likely to order light, which means four vodka tonics. Her pupils dilated, her speech patterns repetitive and frenzied, she'll clutch your arm in one hand and a cigarette in the other as she talks about how goddamn fabulous everyone is, and how things have never been better or more interesting. David Bowie! She would love to f-ing hear some Bowie right now. Can someone make that happen? Anyway. You were saying? But you weren't saying. Anything. And you probably won't, for the rest of the night, until the sparkly magic runs its course and she becomes sullen and shaky and you must physically remove her from your place lest she call her delivery guy again.

WHAT TO DO

Never borrow her jeans, her car, or her handbag. And if things get bad, coax her to rehab with tales of how many celebrities she'll meet there!

the still-friends-with-your-ex-boyfriend friend

HABITAT: Your ex's place of employment, graduate school, tennis club

IDENTIFYING CHARACTERISTICS: Is friends with him

PRO: She knows if he's seeing someone, and who the little tramp is

CON: Extracting good details is maddeningly impossible

CATCHPHRASE: "How *are* you?"

Let's face it: The SFWYEBF is not your friend. She's merely a carrier pigeon for relaying information about your post-breakup awesomeness to your ex—while at the same time reporting back information about his current state of (here's hoping) misery. The problems, of course, are that you don't know if she's withholding information from you at his request or out of fear of hurting your feelings, and this feels demeaning, somehow; like parents spelling out the word "C-O-O-K-I-E" instead of saying it, so the toddler doesn't throw a fit. You'll get only hazy details. Ski house? Is he in on the ski house? With what snow bunny . . . or bunnies? If she does let it slip that he's dating, in a LTR, or, gulp, engaged, it may be the end of your friendship. Even though you're not supposed to kill the messenger, you might never get over the urge to throttle her.

WHAT TO DO

Whenever you hang out with her, you always must be fabulous, blithe, gorgeous, and over it . . . which, of course, you are.

the so-slammed-at-work-right-now friend

HABITAT: *Still* at work!

IDENTIFYING CHARACTERISTICS: Fancy pants, rumpled blouse, multiple wireless communication devices

PRO: Her work ethic is inspiring; she picks up the check

CON: You get it—she's busy

CATCHPHRASE: Uses!! Lots!!! Of exclamation points!!!

She is so slammed right now. Work has been crazy. Insane. Seriously! She hasn't been to the gym in like . . . wait, can you hold on? She's gotta go. It's her boss. She'll-call-you-back-later-OK? Click. Dial tone. This is likely the most meaningful interaction you'll ever have with the So-Slammed-at-Work-Right-Now Friend. You'll leave up to ten voicemails and roughly as many e-mails and texts before she gets back to you, and when she does, the message is always the same: *I am so slammed right now!* Take a deep breath and try not to take her human-hold-music routine personally. It's hard, though, because beyond the indignity of being ignored, there's often a hint of self-righteousness in her harried tone, indicating that you, lazy grad student or entry-level drone, *couldn't possibly comprehend* how busy a person with her myriad responsibilities actually is. When, in truth, you can comprehend it. Because she tells you about it. Every day.

WHAT TO DO

Stop trying to contact her. When things are "less crazy" she'll come around. Then act busy!

wireless communication devices

rumpled blouse

fancy pants

paper avalanche

the smack-talking friend

HABITAT: Empty bathroom, in line at salad bar, proximate bar stool

IDENTIFYING CHARACTERISTICS: Friendly countenance tempered by wicked gleam in eye

PRO: Allows you to vent copiously without judgment

CON: You talk a lot more smack than usual

CATCHPHRASE: "Give me the goods!"

Some friendships are formed by an alliance against a mutual enemy. In this case, that enemy is another friend. Your time with the Smack-Talking Friend will be spent talking all sorts of smack about a third party not present. The object of your mutual disdain might be pretentious and haughty, unabashedly slutty, uptight and unyielding, judgmental, or psychotic. But you begin to relish your encounters with this bête noire, because she provides you fresh fodder. You and the STF will sit down, blandly discuss elements of your respective lives, and then suddenly talk switches to Her for a shot of conversational adrenaline. Anecdotes are exchanged, gestures are imitated, nicknames are developed, hypotheses are thrown around. The problem is that when you run out of smack-talking steam, you may find a void, like when the last of the booze runs out and you realize that's all you really had in common. And that is sad.

WHAT TO DO

To smack talk is human. To not smack talk is divine.
It's a lot easier to be human.

the brilliantly bitchy IM friend

HABITAT: Next cube over

IDENTIFYING CHARACTERISTICS: 120 wpm typing, freakishly short attention span, frequent gasps at screen

PRO: You waste a good 60 percent of your day bitching over IM

CON: See above

CATCHPHRASE: "Hahahahahaha!"

Your relationship with the Brilliantly Bitchy IM Friend takes place almost entirely online. She's fast—before you even begin your reply to her IM that your boss is the gayest clown in the gay parade, she's already sub-responding with a JPEG of a gay clown in a gay parade. Her electronic vitriol is a bittersweet escape, and over time, you will develop a dialogue that bears as little resemblance to the English language as ancient Tagalog, with constantly evolving acronyms and ironic emoticons replacing actual figures of speech. This being the case, your face-to-face time with the Brilliantly Bitchy IM Friend will be a bit awkward. Though her online vernacular may be wickedly insightful, she may have trouble effectively communicating with a live person. She has a tendency to T&T (text and talk) that you may find infuriating. Even if you're able to wrest the phone from her hand, it's no use: You can see her eyes dancing around your face, looking desperately for the refresh button.

WHAT TO DO

Keep in touch. You don't really have a choice, do you?

the secretly-
still-a-virgin friend

HABITAT: Second-hand bookstores, Pixar movies, duck ponds

IDENTIFYING CHARACTERISTICS: Wide-legged jeans, vests, un-ironic bangs

PRO: Is pure and innocent

CON: You can never talk about anything vaguely sexual

CATCHPHRASE: "It just didn't feel right."

When it comes to losing one's virginity, there's the ideal (at a secluded beach house with your sensitive hottie boyfriend, Jake Ryan) and there's the reality (3 A.M., your date is fumbling with the condom, ow-ow-ow, done). Point being: It's not as if this friend is missing out on the Best of Times, but forfeiting one's virginity does hold much significance. You've been there, as has most everyone in your peer group, but she hasn't. And the desire not to make her feel bad coupled with the confused fascination as to how she got to be twenty-eight without doing the deed lends an unsettling anthropological bent to your interactions. The Secretly-Still-a-Virgin Friend never discusses her sex life—just nods mutely if the conversation veers toward the intimate. You're torn between assuming it's a moral decision and wondering whether to fill her with tequila and head to a rugby party.

WHAT TO DO

Keep tabs on SSAV. Once she finally does do it, she's going to become a rabid sex fiend, and that's always entertaining!

un-ironic bangs

duck pond

vest

wide-legged jeans

unisex footwear

the friend-you-met-that-summer-you-worked-at-Chili's friend

HABITAT: Random Midwestern suburb or resort town

IDENTIFYING CHARACTERISTICS: Perky red polo shirt, black half-apron, flair

PRO: That summer was SO crazy!

CON: That was ten years ago

CATCHPHRASE: "I want my baby-back-baby-back-baby-back ribs!"

So, there was that one summer between sophomore and junior year when you weren't in the mood for the assistant paralegal job your dad had hooked up, but still needed cash. You drove the streets of your hometown, desolate and depressed, until you came across the red chili pepper of opportunity—a waitress job. You bonded with one girl immediately, who shared your mortification at serving Crispy Honey-Chipotle Chicken Crispers™ to your former classmates. You spent your shifts making fun of customers and ogling Tim the bartender, who'd slip you El Niño margaritas in the guise of a plastic mug of strawberry lemonade. You'd sneak out for smoke breaks, verbally joust with the kitchen staff, and blow all of your tips on drinks at Crogan's, the Chilis-like establishment across the street. You did some crazy things, but today it's hard to dig up what you have in common besides ranch-dip–soaked memories.

WHAT TO DO

Think of her every time you have anything boneless and fried, which might be more often than you'd like to admit.

the territorial friend

HABITAT: Scrolling through your text messages, Blackberry, and e-mail account

IDENTIFYING CHARACTERISTICS: Flared nostrils, claw-like manicure

PRO: Passive

CON: Aggressive

CATCHPHRASE: "You invited her? Oh."

The TTF is your best friend. She values your charm, validates your taste, and thinks you're true kindred spirits . . . until you casually invite your friend Jen to the beach one weekend, and suddenly you're a heartless bitch. The Territorial Friend stealthily monitors your social life like a film noir private eye, and if you show any signs of preferential treatment toward another friend, she will freak out, usually in the form of a cutting little e-mail or series of texts: "Sounds like you're really busy. Hope you had fun at the beach w/your best friend Jen. See you next year." Reasoning with a fuming Territorial Friend isn't an option, so you must instead take her out to a nice dinner and begrudgingly downplay Jen's coolness all night. Or there's the riskier—but recommended—route of rebuffing her seventh grade tactics with a withering comeback: "Don't worry, you're still the #1 speed dial on my Swatch phone."

WHAT TO DO

Consider phasing her out, slowly but subtly.
Imagine what she'll do once you get a boyfriend . . .

threat level orange
The High-Risk Friend

This friend tends to be self-involved, self-righteous, or plain old-fashioned selfish. Since the primary qualification of friendship is forgoing the self in the spirit of camaraderie and giving, she does not represent the ideal companion. Simply put, Threat Level Orange is like too much fake tanner: never good.

the non-
confrontational friend
(AKA THE E-MAILS OF RAGE FRIEND)

HABITAT: At home in her room, "working late" at the office

IDENTIFYING CHARACTERISTICS: Laptop, furrowed brow

PRO: Is sweet and affable

CON: Until you open your e-mail

CATCHPHRASE: "NO SUBJECT"

The Non-Confrontational Friend can never express a negative emotion. She avoids conflict, defusing it with a smile, a joke, an unnecessary apology. She squeezes her rage into a bitter little package, wraps it up with a tight satin ribbon, and puts it in mental storage. Until she opens her e-mail browser. And all of the things she wishes she'd said, all of the injustices, come out in a poorly punctuated deluge of e-disgust. It's so harsh, and so indelible, and so unexpected that you quite often don't know how to respond. A succinct "I'm sorry" is often a better tactic than trying to point-counterpoint her angry missive, which will just result in another laborious e-mail picking apart the inconsistencies in your argument. You may be tempted to forward this e-mail to other friends, but be extremely careful. You're just one mistaken REPLY ALL away from the destruction of your friendship.

WHAT TO DO

Tell her your server is down, and watch her e-rage dissolve as she tries to describe it in real time.

the foodie friend

HABITAT: Greenmarket, James Beard Society meeting, Whole Foods produce section

IDENTIFYING CHARACTERISTICS: Copies of *Cooks Illustrated*, short fingernails, clogs

PRO: Cooks a mean coq au vin

CON: Spends the entire dinner telling you how

CATCHPHRASE: "It's in firm-ball stage!"

Happily basking in the newfound caché of the culinary world, the Foodie Friend uses terms like "farm to table" as though she'd come up with the idea herself. When she goes to the farmer's market—at 8 A.M., every Saturday, rain or shine—she gets into lengthy discussions with vendors about soil gradients, nodding sagely as though she's a grizzled old farmhand and not an upwardly mobile urbanite. Her dinner parties are a thing of shock and awe. They require weeks of preparation and menus that call not just for central valley artichokes, but ones from Blue Moon Farms, the fourth row from the left. Engaging her in a discussion concerning anything hand-churned is risky, but she's particularly manic on cheeses. If she invites you over for a wine and cheese tasting, do not eat too much of the cheese. Even though you're hungry, and it's a tasting, dammit, the sight of you wolfing down $18 worth of Marin Cowgirl Creamery Red Label causes her physical pain.

WHAT TO DO

Tell her to eat, drink, and perhaps get a life.

the aggressively
christian friend

HABITAT: Soup kitchens, concerts by bands you've never heard of, exurban Arizona

IDENTIFYING CHARACTERISTICS: Turtleneck, gold cross, nude hose with flats

PRO: So nice and giving

CON: So judgmental and scary!

CATCHPHRASE: "WWJD?"

The Aggressively Christian Friend is not necessarily out to convert your immortal soul through His Word and marshmallow casseroles, but that said, it's a little uncomfortable knowing that she's so very down with the Lord. It's really difficult to change the subject once somebody says "Jesus" or opens up a pocket Bible and announces there's something you should hear. Sometimes she'll ask you questions that you just don't want to answer. "Do you mind if I say grace?" "Are you sure you don't want to come to Youth Group tonight?" "Do you really think another drink is the answer?" Your response to all may be a resounding "yes!" but instead you just give her the shrug of the damned. Although you might consider tempering your more salacious anecdotes with milder conversational fare, you shalt not feel like less of a person just because you prefer the Cup of Noodles to the Cup of Christ.

WHAT TO DO

Let's get real, here. She went one way, you went another.
Blame your heathen parents.

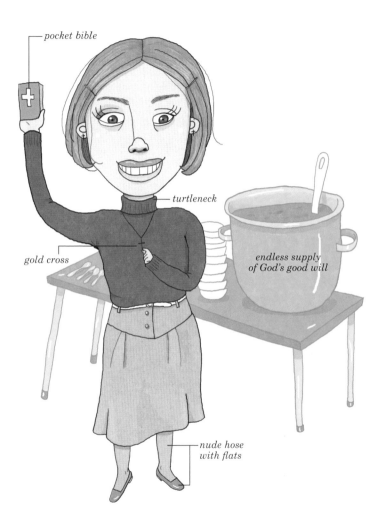

pocket bible

turtleneck

gold cross

endless supply
of God's good will

nude hose
with flats

the "I'm from New York" friend

HABITAT: Downtown, Gramercy, LES	
IDENTIFYING CHARACTERISTICS: Expensive boots, loud, nasally accent, razor-cut bob	
PRO: Sophisticated	
CON: Tries too hard	
CATCHPHRASE: "You call this pizza?"	

The "I'm from New York" Friend never tires of reminding you where she lives and why it's superior in every way. From the "culture" to the "energy" to the public transportation, it's the Greatest City in the World! Mentioning that you have actually been to this electrifying city and tried the pizza and don't think it's that great results in a sigh, a snort, and a shrug that says: "Only real New Yorkers get it." The thing is, this friend is *not* a real New Yorker, having moved there only after college. Still, she's quick to work her adopted hometown into every conversation: "Well, I'm from New York and we don't put up with that BS!" she'll crow, or "My apartment is the size of your closet, but hey, in New York you go out all the time!" It sure sounds like a nice place, and you sure wish she'd go back there.

WHAT TO DO

Remain friendly, since you might need a place to stay. And try to get her to admit she was born in Spokane, or even better, Canada.

the cheap friend

HABITAT: Albertsons, Payless, Macy's on Columbus Day

IDENTIFYING CHARACTERISTICS: The cute blandness of the rigorous discount shopper

PRO: A model of restraint and prudence

CON: Wine by the glass

CATCHPHRASE: "I'm really trying to budget right now."

More than frugal, the Cheap Friend is just plain cheap. You can't go to dinner with her without bringing a calculator, and woe to you if you choose her as a roommate: everything from a 49-cent sponge to your slice count from a late-night pizza will be itemized and placed neatly on the fridge for you to contribute your share. Cheap Friend is otherwise a kind soul, but when it comes to cash she suddenly turns into a ruthless negotiator, haggling relentlessly with the hippie woman at the farmers' market. It's not that she's particularly financially downtrodden (she may have a steady job or trust fund), but pinching pennies is simply her way of staying in control. Never shop with this girl or you'll face a retail experience that includes a giant, fluorescent-lit communal changing pen, where the sight of a morbidly obese 70-year-old in control hose will effectively terminate any desire you had to get dressed in the first place.

WHAT TO DO

Do *not* invite her to your birthday dinner.

the megalomaniac hostess friend

HABITAT: High-end florist, stationery store, soup tureen convention

IDENTIFYING CHARACTERISTICS: Hand-embroidered apron, whisk, look of manic concern

PRO: Throws a kickass baby shower

CON: Almost has a coronary doing it

CATCHPHRASE: "Is the Frangelico chilled? *It must be chilled!*"

The Megalomaniac Hostess is a particular glutton for punishment, insisting on throwing intensely elaborate parties for occasions large and small, with an attention to detail that borders on obsessive-compulsiveness. For her Butterfly Garden Party, there will not just be butterfly-shaped ice in the punch bowl, but hand-carved butterfly soaps in the guest bathroom, butterfly-embossed napkins, butterfly-shaped quiches, butterfly-shaped butter pats, hanging handmade iridescent butterflies, and individual butterfly-shaped place cards that spell out each guest's name, in tiny butterflies. She will have set up two separate omelet stations, home-brewed iced tea in three freshly squeezed seasonal flavors, and midway through the gathering she'll sneak off to the home and garden store for fresh sod because the dirt under the stone pathway to the garden party doesn't look "brown enough." Any attempts to assist the MH will result in a tart, "No thank you, please just enjoy the party!" accompanied by a grimace that sends you running from the kitchen.

WHAT TO DO

Hang in there. You totally want to be invited to her wedding.

look of manic concern

cake too perfect to eat

hand-embroidered apron

freshly-laid hardscaping

the naked friend

HABITAT: Anywhere, anytime

IDENTIFYING CHARACTERISTICS: Naked

PRO: Is very comfortable with her body

CON: Maybe too comfortable

CATCHPHRASE: "Can I borrow your tweezers?"

Naked Friend doesn't see nudity as a big deal and has no problem going topless while sunbathing. Not on a beach in Corsica, mind you, but in your parents' backyard. If you dare go to the gym with Naked Friend, she'll peel off her clothes and begin applying lotion, sitting cross-legged on a bench, chatting up a storm as you nervously avert your eyes. Whether in your apartment or summer-share beach house, she has a habit of exiting the shower, taking the towel you had placed pointedly on a hook, wrapping it around her head, and striding purposefully around, oblivious to everyone's awkward silence. It would be one thing if she were a "Free to Be," grew-up-in-a-naked-house-variety hippie girl, but she's usually toned and groomed to the hilt, suggesting that she's flaunting her physique to attract admiration and jealousy . . . when really all she's attracting is profound discomfort.

WHAT TO DO

For her next birthday, give her a nice fluffy bathrobe and see if it takes.

the boyfriend mind meld friend

(AKA THE "DAN SEZ" FRIEND)

HABITAT: Over at Dan's!

IDENTIFYING CHARACTERISTICS: Dan's Cornell sweatshirt

PRO: Dan has some interesting opinions once in awhile

CON: A long while

CATCHPHRASE: "Dan says corporations are bad!"

Most girls, at some point in their lives, get so swept up in the emotional tidal wave of a new or especially thrilling relationship that they essentially forfeit their personalities. They usually get them back, but with this girl, it happens all the time, and she doesn't. Whichever guy she's dating, she molds herself to fit the specific parameters of his lifestyle, adopting his cultural preferences and sports team affiliations. She also says his name a lot. It's Dan says this, Dan was saying that. Most sentences will begin with "Dan and I . . ." and then culminate in some Dan-related story that has neither relevance nor humor value. This friend will often repeat herself, so dazzled is she by the fascinating World of Dan. "Yeah, you already mentioned that Dan says Thule bike racks are the best," you'll say. To which she'll cheerfully retort, "Oh Dan says I repeat myself all the time and it drives people crazy!" For once, Dan is right.

WHAT TO DO

Forget her. Dan is all she needs.

the marginally famous friend

HABITAT: Obscure promotional events, Sundance, Business Class

IDENTIFYING CHARACTERISTICS: $5,400 bag, suspiciously stiff facial expressions

PRO: Has a bit of that "I'm famous" effervescence

CON: A lot of that is just the drugs

CATCHPHRASE: "I'll see if I can get you on the list."

Either employed by a major celebrity (assistant, personal chef, private yoga instructor, random lackey) or a minor celebrity in her own right (Bravo reality show contestant, catalogue model), this friend is a satellite in the outer orbits of the fame-o-sphere. Between halfhearted inquiries about your life and times, she'll casually let slip certain details of her "fabulous" life that usually involve designer brand purchases or former *Real World* cast members. She will be on her BlackBerry the rest of the time, gasping occasionally and then saying, "Sorry, it's just . . ." But you are not famous enough for her to finish the sentence. Once in awhile she'll invite you to an exciting event, and you'll go backstage and find yourself introduced as "my great friend!" to people who look glazed and bored to be talking to a friend-of-a-marginally-famous-person.

WHAT TO DO

She will either get too famous and move on, or have a sad downward spiral and get her real estate license.

the undercover slut friend

HABITAT: Beach parties, Schrager hotel lobbies, any given mall

IDENTIFYING CHARACTERISTICS: Low-rise jeans, halter, hair blown-out within an inch of its life

PRO: Is sexy and daring

CON: Is a bit of a slut

CATCHPHRASE: "Hey, babe!"

This friend is frankly promiscuous, in an understated way. Sounds impossible? Well, she is. Although she may score quite low on the hoochie-o-meter, she does have the unnerving ability to suddenly turn up the sexy-sexy in any situation. You might bring her along to a seemingly innocuous activity—mini golf, a cooking class—but when a good-looking guy appears on the horizon she'll turn from good-natured companion to Tawny Kitaen. Her posture will change, a finger will play on her bottom lip, she'll stop joking with you and start teasing him until suddenly you feel like an extra in a soft-core movie that *you never ordered*. The worst part about the USF is that she can so easily slide back into your normal pal, so if you protest to your significant other about her wily ways, he'll just tell you to relax and stop acting jealous. Then he'll ask you to invite her over for a beer.

WHAT TO DO

Sometimes it's good to have a slutty friend. *Sometimes*.

the insanely paranoid friend

HABITAT: Self-defense class, Neighborhood Watch meeting, well-lit locations

IDENTIFYING CHARACTERISTICS: Pepper spray, antibacterial wipes, giant handbag clutched to chest

PRO: Worries enough for the both of you

CON: Needs a police escort after 5 P.M.

CATCHPHRASE: "Can you walk me to my car?"

The Insanely Paranoid Friend watched too many after-school specials as a young girl. She's convinced that everyone, from the geeky pizza delivery teen to your accountant, is a menacing criminal out to rape, rob, and pillage. And she is not subtle. "Is this a safe neighborhood?" she'll ask, loudly, if any male not attired in pressed khakis and a blazer walks by. She refuses to take public transportation and will never let anyone buy her a drink. If a homeless person asks her for change, she will shake her head violently and run—not walk—to the other side of the street, calling her mom on her cell and relating the incident en route. At work, at family picnics, and at dinner parties, she takes her purse with her to the bathroom. If you try to joke with her about her overprotective ways, she'll start reciting violent crime statistics, which will assault-and-batter any cocktail party conversation into oblivion.

WHAT TO DO

Be sympathetic, but don't indulge her paranoia.
And don't invite her on your trip to Mardi Gras.

well-lit location

pepper spray

giant handbag

own shadow

the blogger friend

HABITAT: Cross-legged on ergonomic chair, Apple Store, the "cool" coffee shop

IDENTIFYING CHARACTERISTICS: American Apparel, ironic '80s sunglasses, snarky disposition

PRO: Produces searing electronic insights into pop cultural phenomena and specifics of her sexual escapades

CON: See above

CATCHPHRASE: "He's on my blogroll!"

In the olden days, the Blogger Friend would be the Dear Diary Friend—the pretty, smart-alecky girl with Peppermint Patty glasses who carried a tattered notebook everywhere, diligently recording every thought and feeling, from the hypocrisy of gym teachers to the bottomless intensity of her feelings for Justin Barrett, the sensitive sophomore poet/water-polo player. Nothing much has changed, except now she's doing it in public, broadcasting her snarky opinions, party photos, and thinly disguised romantic exploits to thousands of strangers via Livejournal or Blogspot. It's fine, but it's also a little irritating: the assumption that you should care that she finds this book or that movie overrated or expects you to find enrichment by reading her self-indulgent takes on love. The worst is when she produces "blind items" that clearly identify the guy she's dating and then chronicles their inevitable breakup in painful detail. You feel grossed out, like you're reading her diary. Which in a way, Dear Reader, you are.

WHAT TO DO

Set your status to "unavailable."
After all, you don't want her posting about *you*.

the "let's go to Vegas!" friend

HABITAT: Bikini wax place, the club, Southwest Airlines

IDENTIFYING CHARACTERISTICS: Juicy jumpsuit, Dior sunglasses, rum-and-Coke and/or large iced Starbucks beverage

PRO: Attracts hot guys

CON: Attracts hot guys who dig the jumpsuit

CATCHPHRASE: G-L-A-M-O-R-O-U-S Yeah!

This friend spends a lot of time in Vegas. She's not a gambler, and she's not there to see Cirque du Soleil or Celine or to dine at Laurent Tourondel's new place. She just loves to party 24/7 and hang out with "players," who may or may not be midlevel software salesmen from Tempe in town for a conference. What LGTV lacks in common sense she makes up for in her ability to drink multiple mojitos before noon and chew gum, smoke, talk on her cell phone, and play slots at the same time. Sure, she's sort of tacky, but in her company you'll rediscover the PussyCat Dolls musical oeuvre, learn how to work a nightclub stripper pole, and likely end up in an ensuite Jacuzzi. However, your kinship is hindered by the knowledge that it's just a matter of time before LGTV scarfs down a handful of MDMA in your shared room at the Palms and tries to sleep with your boyfriend. Or, possibly, you.

WHAT TO DO

Start spending weekends at museums or chamber music concerts in lieu of Vegas. You'll never hear from her again.

the girly girl friend

HABITAT: Antique store, Anthropologie, Cinderella's Castle

IDENTIFYING CHARACTERISTICS: Awful shoes, Mary Engelbreit calendar, diamond heart pendant

PRO: Non-threatening, sweet

CON: Kitten calendar

CATCHPHRASE: [Girlish squeal]

The Girly Girl Friend is really into being a girl. She clings to a musty, dated notion of femininity that spooks you, even as it acts as a palliative against the harsh realities of the modern world. She reads Jane Austen books, has Winnie-the-Pooh bedding, and curls up with a hot cup of cocoa when life throws her a curveball. She loves old movies, especially with a plucky young heroine who finds true love, and she cries at the drop of a hat. *Do not* get her started on her dog or cat. Alive or dead, the mere mention of Sadie or Li'l Bits will illicit hours of ruminations on his or her special comforts. She wears braids, pastels, and pearl earrings, works in education or the arts, and considers Ziggy edgy. Advanced Girly Girl Friends are afraid of most boys and have never made out with one, due to a proliferation of antique doll and stuffed animal collections crowding her bed and a staunch aversion to malt beverages.

WHAT TO DO

Drift apart at will. Know, however, that you will break her heart.

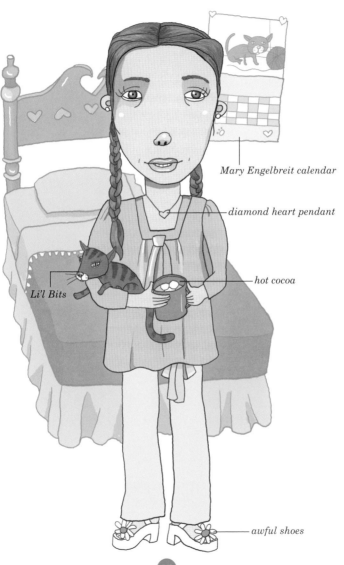

Mary Engelbreit calendar

diamond heart pendant

hot cocoa

Li'l Bits

awful shoes

the flaky friend

HABITAT: At home, stuck at work, at a family obligation, laid up with a migraine, just taking care of a few things, on the other line . . .

IDENTIFYING CHARACTERISTICS: Jittery air of flakiness, unwillingness to commit to anything, ever

PRO: That's one less for dinner . . .

CON: . . . your rehearsal dinner.

CATCHPHRASE: "I am *so* sorry, but. . ."

The Flaky Friend is inconsiderate, spacey, and either a social recluse or a social climber, but she *is* consistent. Like clockwork, she will manage to opt out of any gathering, selecting one excuse from what seems to be a preordained list: "I hurt my leg at the gym." "Car trouble." "I have a peanut allergy." "The cat is making a wheezing sound." "It's my cousin's birthday." Technology makes this exchange even easier. Texting "Bronchitis!" is a lot easier than faking a deep chest cold. Even excuses are unnecessary, for she has perfected the art of the quasi-commitment: "I'll try to make it." The good news is that you can maintain a close friendship with this person without ever actually seeing her. Entire years may go by where plans are made and then flaked upon. Pretty soon the thought of actually meeting up with her fills you with a sense of irrational dread—what will you have to talk about?—coupled with relief when she does, inevitably, flake.

WHAT TO DO

Stop making plans and nature will take its course.

the bookish hipster friend

HABITAT: Public library, author readings, vintage bike shop

IDENTIFYING CHARACTERISTICS: Bangs, New Balance sneakers, moleskin notebook

PRO: Pals with Dave Eggers

CON: Exclusionary and lit-snobbish

CATCHPHRASE: "I have several projects in the works right now."

This is the girl for whom the word "twee" was invented. Serious yet self-consciously dreamy and always too-cool-for-school, she is part of the new wave of post-post-modernist literature lovers who consider four pages of doodles, charts, and bullet points the creative equivalent of a Dostoyevsky death scene. She takes her writing very, very seriously. If you are to invite her over to your place, you must hide all evidence of chick lit, John Grisham, or wayward copies of *Cosmo*. She rolls with a crowd of people who uniformly wear black-frame glasses, carry messenger bags, have shaggy hair, hang out in free-trade coffee shops, and consider themselves radically individualistic. She believes in the power of childlike wonder and the employment of Foucault quotes in casual conversation. The combination of quasi-literary pretension and do-goodedness is enough to make her personal letterpress dodo-bird logo choke on its own smugness.

WHAT TO DO

Pass on her next reading. And her loft-warming party. And her art show. The End.

the pro sports fan friend

HABITAT: Tailgate, sports bar, applying lipstick in stadium bathroom

IDENTIFYING CHARACTERISTICS: Baby-T with cute pastel rendering of sports team logo, or old-school jersey and hat

PRO: Teaches you the difference between a slider and a split-finger fastball

CON: You don't really care

CATCHPHRASE: "YEAH BABY! WOOO!"

The Pro Sports Fan Friend knows the players, keeps track of the trades, paints her face in the post-season, and gets really into televised games, calling out players by nickname and swearing heartily at the ref or umpire. This lets guys know that she is not one of those girls who adopts a fake interest for tacit male approval. She is hardcore. She is *down*. She'll usually use the first person possessive, e.g., "*My* Sox" or "*My* Packers." She'll throw out stats and argue with the guys about this pitcher's ERA or that running back's yardage, and although you've got to admire her team spirit, you wish she'd simmer down, have a drink, and talk about something of substance, like which young celebrity got a DUI/knocked up/gay this weekend. Guys find her a novelty but after a while some may get sick of her constant need to prove herself and tune her out in favor of the more genial commentary of Terry Bradshaw.

WHAT TO DO

Let's Go! Away!

giant foam finger

face paint

sports team
beer cozy

old-school jersey

tailgating props

the crazy cat lady friend

HABITAT: Searching for the can opener

IDENTIFYING CHARACTERISTICS: Draggy skirt, Meow Mix scent

PRO: Is a caring, loving parent

CON: Of cats

CATCHPHRASE: "You won't believe what Butterscotch did!"

The Crazy Cat Lady Friend was once just a normal friend with a comfortable apartment and active social life, but somewhere down the line things went horribly awry. She has no qualms about discussing her cats' social machinations as if they're mutual friends. "Tally did the most adorable thing the other day! She and Mookie were fighting, and then she did that thing with her rump where she kind of, you know, twitches it around and . . ." At this point you may have lost consciousness. Her apartment is a hot zone of crazy-cat-lady fallout, from the suspiciously furry couch and giant carpeted "cat condo" where the TV used to be, to the litter box seated disconcertingly in the bathroom. Even though her unconditional devotion to her feline friends speaks of a kind soul with a lot of love to give, few men will make it through the door without mentally transmogrifying her into a *Cathy* comic. Or even worse, *Garfield*.

WHAT TO DO

Take some Benadryl and try to maintain friendly relations.

the girlfriend-of-your-platonic-guy-friend friend

HABITAT: At your Platonic Guy Friend's place. Always.

IDENTIFYING CHARACTERISTICS: Staring daggers at you while stroking his chest, defiantly

PRO: Pretty and perceptive

CON: Controlling and threatened

CATCHPHRASE: "This has been really fun, but [Platonic Guy Friend] and I have an early day, so . . . "

You have a Platonic Guy Friend—meaning you've never hooked up, not even after the infamous Night of 14 Margaritas. This solid fact notwithstanding, your Platonic Guy Friend's girlfriend hates you. Big time. You can't really blame her—you're the cute, laid-back sidekick, drinking beers and eating chicken wings with him in the middle of the day, while she's either at turbo Pilates or busy telling him he's late for something. To overcome this imbalance, she resorts to flank attacks, criticizing your clothes ("that's a brave look!"), your grooming ("I see the 'natural eyebrow' is coming back!"), and your intellect ("Florida State—wasn't that your alma mater?"), making time spent with your Platonic Guy Friend uncomfortable. But as you have no stake in the Platonic Guy Friend's affections, the GOYPGF is ultimately harmless, and there is much fun to be had in being perceived as a threatening temptress—as well as priceless insight into how transparent female jealousy really is. Take notes.

WHAT TO DO

Don't let her get to you—but look smokin' hot at their wedding.

threat level red
The Severe-Risk Friend

This girl is duplicitous, demonic, delusional, debauched, demeaning, depressive, and an all-around D- on the friendship report card. She is to be avoided at all times, at all costs. Don't make plans to see her, screen all her calls, and if you do run into her in some unlucky gin joint, the operative phrase is RUN LIKE HELL.

the too-cool friend

HABITAT: The part of town that isn't ruined by gentrification

IDENTIFYING CHARACTERISTICS: Mix of couture, thrift, and
Too-Cool Boyfriend's outerwear

PRO: Elevates your own cultural awareness

CON: Leaves you feeling deflated and mad

CATCHPHRASE: "I don't really believe in catchphrases."

She's cooler than you. You know it, she knows it. You don't mind playing second fiddle in the alt-country band that is her life, but it does grate, especially when her signifiers of cool often seem so . . . obvious. For instance, you would never exclaim, "Ooh, Belle & Sebastien B-sides!" But she does, and then it's like you're a loser for not getting it. When you do! It happens every time: You overestimate her coolness, she underestimates yours, and together you grimly endure the missed pop-culture references and strained silences. In conversation she makes you do all the work as she stares down at her fingerless gloves and sighs. The Too-Cool Friend is rarely seen without her Too-Cool Boyfriend, who regards you with an unappetizing mix of pity and scorn and overcompensates by acting super interested in what you're saying—when really he's mentally blogging about the tragedy of the American public school system that produced you.

WHAT TO DO

Start a gradual but firm fade-out. This will make you seem more aloof and, thus, more cool. You win!

the creepy clinger friend

HABITAT: Right by your side

IDENTIFYING CHARACTERISTICS: Slight build, pale features, wringing hands

PRO: You'll never roam alone

CON: Holds your hand in public

CATCHPHRASE: "Where are you going?"

The Creepy Clinger Friend has a few issues with self-esteem and boundaries: She doesn't have either. In high-stakes social situations, she clings to you with the blindness of a newborn possum. She stands a little too close, laughs a little too hard, and always, always, accompanies you to the bathroom even if she does nothing but stare at the outdated tampon dispenser as you use the facilities. She is nearly impossible to shake. She'll call, text, and IM, asking what your plans are for the evening and forcing her way into your night's agenda. You may feel trapped and enraged, but when she offers to buy you a drink, be the designated driver, or sweet talk the bouncer so you get a banquette, your anger melts. This reconciliation tends to be short-lived, because CC doesn't get the message to back off; instead she sits beside you, pointlessly piggybacking on every joke or statement you make, silently, creepily, watching you.

WHAT TO DO

Like an emergency amputation, a sudden severing of all contact is painful but necessary.

the best-friends-since-fourth-grade friend

HABITAT: Birthdays, weddings, significant life events

IDENTIFYING CHARACTERISTICS: Looks the same, only different

PRO: Knows you so well

CON: Makes you feel like you're twelve

CATCHPHRASE: "Remember when . . . ?"

There are two distinct types of Best-Friends-Since-Fourth-Grade Friends: the dearest friend ever, with whom you first bonded in Mrs. Bybee's class, and the Original Frenemy, who's been your friend-rival since the day she "accidentally" knocked you off the monkey bars. You tend to remain close with both types because it seems like you have no choice. Your parents are neighbors, you grew up with the same people, and, let's face it, habits are hard to break. If she's a good friend, it's a good thing; if she's a bad friend, it's a very, very bad thing. But therein lies the secret: Just because you've been friends forever does not mean you have to be BFFs forever! If this girl makes you feel helpless or inadequate, brings up embarrassing tales of adolescent awkwardness in front of your new boyfriend, or makes snide comments about your current job ("Retail seems like a great place for you"), cut the cord!

WHAT TO DO

Whichever form this friend takes, heaven-sent or hater, remember that Mrs. Bybee's class is no longer in session.

the flirts-with-every-guy-including-your-dad friend

HABITAT: Forever 21, *Rock of Love* casting call, laser hair removal salon

IDENTIFYING CHARACTERISTICS: Gravelly laugh, enormous rack, several layers of lip gloss, no underwear

PRO: When not flirting, can be fun and insightful

CON: Is always flirting

CATCHPHRASE: "Stop it! I'm so ticklish!"

The FWEGIYD Friend is an all-purpose flirt. She's a sucker for male attention of any kind and is brazen in her attempts to provoke it. Whether or not she follows through on these libidinous overtures, you can't introduce her to any guy without her cooing, cajoling, and cleavage flashing until he responds. She employs devices like wearing a kicky cowboy hat to a party, loudly relating how attracted she is to her girlfriends, and rampant lap sitting. She is a particularly lethal force at weddings, birthdays, and any other event where another girl is the center of attention. On these occasions, she goes into flirt-overdrive, luring the DJ, caterer, or groom onto the dance floor for some inappropriate pop-drop-and-lockin' (in many cases, there doesn't even need to be a dance floor). She has a particular yen for older and unavailable men; you'll notice, with disgust, how she'll ask your boyfriend if he's been working out or your dad what his shoe size is. Ewww.

WHAT TO DO

Ditch her while she's riding the mechanical bull.

the "who knew she'd be a bridezilla?" friend

HABITAT: At the hairdresser's for a test-run, veil shopping, anywhere in the vicinity of long-stemmed calla lilies

IDENTIFYING CHARACTERISTICS: Too thin, crazy-eyed, overly plucked

PRO: A cautionary tale about how not to behave on "your day"—or any day

CON: You can't punch the bride

CATCHPHRASE: "I just want it to be perfect!"

The "Who Knew She'd Be a Bridezilla?" Friend betrayed no clues to the monster she would become once the ring was on her finger. The transformation happened virtually overnight. She used to be unpretentious and funny; now she's shelling out $2,000 for Manolo wedding shoes and treating you and your fellow brideslaves as though you're court jesters who are constantly trying her royal patience. In her visions of The Big Day, you're reduced to an accessory like the guest book, there to fill space but never to detract from the main event: her. She talks about her wedding incessantly and turns down any social overture with the lazily articulated excuse of "So much to do!" Then she babbles about the caterer's appalling interpretation of the mini croquettes she saw on *Martha Stewart* and how she feels really bad that you didn't get an "and guest," but seeing as you're not really dating anyone special . . . you understand, right?

WHAT TO DO

Suppress your rage and humiliation by mentally picturing the inevitable Divorce Party Evite.

the bossy friend

HABITAT: Playgrounds, boardrooms, dog-training classes, and other places where she can easily wield authority

IDENTIFYING CHARACTERISTICS: Loud primary colors

PRO: Gets things done

CON: Treats you like an employee

CATCHPHRASE: "We're leaving."

The Bossy Friend chooses the movie, picks the shared appetizers, and decides whom you should date and what you should wear. Your picking anything, from a radio station to a political affiliation, is just *not done* within the confines of your friendship. If you do defy her and, say, go to the restaurant that you suggested—even if the waiters are cuter and the décor cooler and they have your favorite butternut squash ravioli and it's your birthday—she will talk herself into believing it was somehow her idea, or she will boss you into agreeing that her choice would have resulted in a superior dining experience. There will be pouting, then she'll rouse herself to order the waiter around a bit. Interestingly, the bossy friend does not usually make a good boss, saving up all of her real bullying prowess for her close friends and family. You feel sorry for her kids in advance, and hope she never volunteers to coach little league.

WHAT TO DO

Tell her she's no Tony Danza and get outta Dodge!

the self-proclaimed diva friend

HABITAT: Cheesecake Factory, dubious "recording sessions,"
Fake Purse Alley

IDENTIFYING CHARACTERISTICS: Rhinestone-studded tank,
airbrushed nails

PRO: Confident, socially assertive

CON: Deluded, discusses herself in third person

CATCHPHRASE: "They better have Grey Goose."

The Self-Proclaimed Diva Friend dismisses anyone not immediately awed by her fabulousness as "sad and jealous." She'll show up at a relatively tame event wearing knockoff Versace and false eyelashes the size of salad tongs, but what really makes her stand out is the awesome force of her desperation, surrounding her like a cloud of off-brand musk. She considers herself very talented and destined to be a star but has never proven this in any substantive way, other than belting out off-key Christina Aguilera in her leased convertible. It goes without saying that the Self-Proclaimed Diva loves drama. She picks fights with service professionals, forcing you to mediate, calmly explaining that the waitress was only asking if she was finished with her entrée, not calling her fat or unimportant. Another tactic is to distract her with a shiny object, like her bedazzled Sidekick, which she will then use to rapidly text her series of shady boyfriends, whom she refers to only by initials.

WHAT TO DO

Take this high-maintenance friend to the shop—and
leave her there.

the sorta racist friend

HABITAT: Wine bars, country clubs, Kentucky Derby

IDENTIFYING CHARACTERISTICS: Nautica wear, BMW, flinty self-satisfied countenance

PRO: Tells good jokes

CON: Has heart of darkness

CATCHPHRASE: "He's, you know, black."

Uh-oh. Did she just say that? Yes, she did. The Sorta Racist Friend can be difficult to identify at first. It's not as though she casually mentions that all Puerto Ricans should be sterilized at birth, but she does exude just a shade of an evil-racist person, letting you know that it's not such a tolerant world, after all. If you relate that your roommate complains about having to buy the toilet paper all the time, she will say, lightly, and with no inflection, "Erin is Jewish, right?" That's it. Right there. Or maybe she'll repeat a story about an incident at the drycleaners and do the crazy-ethnic-accent-stereotype-voice in a way that is not cool. Don't let her off the hook. The next time she makes one of her evil bon mots, give her a dead stare and say, "*In*appropriate." Or the more colorful, "That's enough out of you, Xenophobia, Warrior Princess."

WHAT TO DO

Give her the boot. The problem is not going to get better as she ages, marries a guy named Chad, moves to a wealthy suburb, and her world exponentially narrows.

the pity junky friend

HABITAT: Doctor's office, emo concert

IDENTIFYING CHARACTERISTICS: Whiny voice, cigarettes, merlot

PRO: Sensitive and in touch with her emotions

CON: So needy and depressing

CATCHPHRASE: "I just don't know what's wrong with me!"

The Pity Junky is addicted to reassurance. Every time you pick up the phone it's another crisis. She had the worst date, the guy made her pay. She had the worst week at work, her cube-mate made fun of her playlist. Why is she so unattractive? Why did her dog have to get a bowel obstruction? Why is her skin so problematic? It dawns on you that she doesn't actually want to be cheered up; she gets high on being a downer. It's exhausting, and you attempt the Fade-Out, but she's impervious to it, showing up at your place at odd hours, monopolizing your couch with her solo pity parties. Soon, you start noticing that you bump into her a lot—running errands, at the library, at the gym. Wait a minute—since when does she belong to your gym? At long last you summon the will to have the Talk with her about the strain she's bringing to your friendship. Let's hope you make it out of that one alive!

WHAT TO DO

Two words: restraining order.

the terminally uptight friend

HABITAT: Ann Taylor Loft, community board meeting, teaching an etiquette seminar

IDENTIFYING CHARACTERISTICS: Linen dresses, minimal makeup, clenched jaw

PRO: Pays the rent on time

CON: Gets offended by the word "damn"

CATCHPHRASE: "That's not funny."

The Terminally Uptight Friend is quietly offended by just about anything. It could be a word choice, a style of dress, or those "gangster-looking" kids snooping around her block. She registers her disapproval with a slight exhale and furrowed brow, and over time you get used to it. Unlike Aggressively Christian Friend, she doesn't have The Lord as an excuse; she just never learned to loosen up. If you wear too much eyeliner she secretly thinks you're a slut; if you allude to smoking pot, you're a degenerate drug addict; and God forbid you divulge any sort of sexual escapade—she'll be inching away from you for fear of catching AIDS, which she is probably convinced has gone airborne. In any social situation, the TU's presence will put you on edge, and you may be inclined to act even more juvenile and scatological as a sort of defense mechanism. Like that time you ordered her a Buttery Nipple shot.

WHAT TO DO

Introduce her to your Crude Friend, sit back, and enjoy your new favorite reality show.

the indie pixie friend

HABITAT: Cupcake store, record shop (vinyl only), anywhere there's PBR

IDENTIFYING CHARACTERISTICS: Under five feet tall, jet-black pixie haircut, white laceless Keds

PRO: Adorable, hip, stylish

CON: You want to crush her like a bug

CATCHPHRASE: "Hey, rockstar."

The Indie Pixie friend trades on her petite stature and edgy style to morph into an adorable mascot of the indie world. She dresses like a punk Rainbow Brite, and from her cranked-up iPod playeth an endless loop of The Knife, Goldfrapp, Dan Deacon, and Feist. Guys, especially a certain breed of anemic Williamsburg guy, love her. *Love* her. It's like a magic formula: little princess + punk chick + fragile female + boy. As a friend, however, she tends to be lost in her own world, and despite her surface sweetness, she is really not to be trusted: If it comes down to you or the bassist, she's going with the bassist. She also has the unnerving ability to make you feel oafish and awkward, so tiny and self-contained is she. You avoid standing next to her at parties for fear of appearing like Gentle Ben. She also has the habit of leaving her iPod in when she talks to you, occasionally drifting off into a closed-eye, head-shaking mini-boogie-down that's truly annoying.

WHAT TO DO

See ya, Tinkerbell.

under five feet tall

jet-black pixie haircut

cranked-up iPod

vinyl records

edgy wardrobe

white laceless Keds

the one-upper friend

HABITAT: Swanky modern condo

IDENTIFYING CHARACTERISTICS: Slightly nicer handbag, slightly taller and thinner, slightly better life

PRO: Keeps you on your toes

CON: This is a friendship, not a competition!

CATCHPHRASE: "I like your coat. Helmut Lang? Oh, wait, Old Navy."

The One-Upper was the girl you grew up with who always had a cuter book bag, always came in first in track, and always asked what grade you got on your Spanish test as she fluttered her *A+! Bueno!* in front of your face. As you grew older, things only got worse: You go to Palm Springs for vacation, she goes to St. Barths. You date an athletic guy, she has a fling with a pro football player. You take a pottery class, she spends a summer in a ceramic residency program in Sicily. It's simply infuriating. And it will never, ever end. You may marry and move to a remote Russian province, and she will still find ways to reach you, reminding you that her life is more varied and inspiring, her husband more handsome and successful, and that she just sold her humorous essay collection for an advance that she classifies as "almost criminal."

WHAT TO DO

Look her up and down and say, "Wow, you're really making headway with that pregnancy weight!" regardless of whether she recently had a child.

the boozy blackout friend

HABITAT: Slumped over a urinal, passed out in Taco Bell drive-through

IDENTIFYING CHARACTERISTICS: Stained shirt, glazed expression

PRO: Wild and crazy

CON: Slappy and sobby

CATCHPHRASE: "Less get annothsher round, bitches!"

At the beginning of the night, Boozy Blackout is jolly good fun, cracking jokes and keeping things lively. By eleven she's grown pensive, taking your hand and telling you what an amazingly awesome friend you are. Come midnight, she's gotta dance, swaying along to Rhianna with her eyes half closed. But when the clock strikes 1 A.M., she goes to the dark side. She hates everyone, including you, her ex, the ex before that, that bitch over there, and the bartender, who seems to be watering down her vodka tonics. Next, you attempt to get her home, which usually results in you hosing out the passenger seat at 2:30 A.M. The final stage occurs at 8 A.M., when she calls you, shakily, for a recap. You may feel reluctant to divulge the details, like the fact that she performed a *Coyote Ugly*–type stomp-dance on the bar or threw up in her new purse, but don't worry—that's what camera phones are for.

WHAT TO DO

Tell her you've quit drinking. Then go to a different bar.

the boring friend

HABITAT: Hardware store, tea house, watching C-Span

IDENTIFYING CHARACTERISTICS: Bland hairstyle, unkempt eyebrows, PBS tote

PRO: Smart and informed

CON: A total snoozefest

CATCHPHRASE: "Yesterday I made egg salad for lunch."

She's sweet, she's steadfast, she's in your corner, and she's . . . so . . . boring! The Boring Friend walks into the room and zaps out all the energy like you've blown a fuse with your hairdryer. She talks in a steady monotone about such scintillating topics as the care and upkeep of her new fiddlehead fern, a suspicious mole on her thigh that needs to be checked out, the copyright infringement lawsuit her boss got in last year, or . . . the . . . zzzzzz. Your friendship poses a moral quandary, because she's intelligent and loyal and never lets you down, but she's like human Ambien. She doesn't understand the difference between anecdote and rote dissertation, and no amount of alcohol will make her even the slightest bit socially engaging—although you certainly try.

WHAT TO DO

Introduce her to your Blabby McBlabberton Friend
and let them talk each other into oblivion.

the fussy vegan friend

HABITAT: Produce section, hiking trail, trendy new religious service

IDENTIFYING CHARACTERISTICS: Recyclable shopping bag, hemp belt, sallow iron-deficient complexion

PRO: Responsible, virtuous, skinny without the aid of diet pills or eating disorders

CON: We're all going to die someday, have a f***ing steak!

CATCHPHRASE: "Sorry, I don't go any higher on the food chain than that."

Guess who's coming to dinner? The Fussy Vegan Friend! So prepare yourself for hours of aggravation. It's not her dietary restrictions; it's the way she presents them as life lessons and moral parables that you are too ignorant or piggish to adhere to. She will email you an exhaustive list of things she can't eat—"no cuttlefish, honey, or buttermilk, please"—that have no relevance to your invitation to Taco Night. Her car bears a "Vegan: Peace for All Who Live!" bumper sticker, which is meant to convey goodwill but really just makes you want to stealthily grind Slim Jims into her macrobiotic brown rice salad. The Fussy Vegan Friend will sometimes offer to bring her own food, but that is just as unsettling, since she produces baggies of rice cheese slices, fava beans, and soy-free meat patties, and shrugs apologetically as she hijacks the kitchen for twenty minutes with her humane gourmet antics.

WHAT TO DO

Congratulate her on her commitment. Then fire up the barbie!

the shallow scenester friend

HABITAT: Dancing, mingling, whispering, playing suggestively with her cocktail straw

IDENTIFYING CHARACTERISTICS: Too much foundation, glaring white veneers

PRO: Seems to love you and genuinely appreciate your personality

CON: Actually hates you

CATCHPHRASE: "So good to see you, sweetie!"

The Shallow Scenester Friend does not have a genuine bone in her body. What she says has no relation to what she actually thinks. "Fabulous dress!" means "Where did you get that rayon-blend mess?" "That's so funny!" means "You suck." The Shallow Scenester flocks to any upscale social scene, whether it's a fashion-forward clubby club or fancy philanthropy. She will speak only to those she regards as equal to or higher than herself status-wise. If she views you as a rival, she will smile brightly and blanket you with BS while scanning for chinks in your armor. She is a charismatic alpha type, and nearly impossible to call out for any of her unseemly traits, because she is also a master of the breezy retort ("Lighten up, babe!"). Although the entertainment industry will embrace her with open arms, she will never have any close girlfriends or experience true intimacy in a relationship.

WHAT TO DO

Wait for her to design a cloddish, trashy fashion line, release an unfortunate R&B single, or marry an octogenarian, and let public opinion do the rest.

too much
foundation

disingenuous
smile

glaring white
veneers

trashy slip dress

alpha-girl stance

killer stilettos

the smelly friend

HABITAT: Essential-oil store, fish market, Salvation Army

IDENTIFYING CHARACTERISTICS: The same brown sweater, every day

PRO: Makes you revisit your college incense phase

CON: Even Lavendar Buddha is powerless against the Smell

CATCHPHRASE: "Why are you sitting all the way over there?"

Do you smell something? Is it a strange, unclassifiable mixture of Lipton onion soup mix, moth balls, and doggie dander? Then your Smelly Friend has arrived, and all will not be well aromatically until a good 20 minutes after she leaves the premises. The Smelly Friend has smelled the same since you were kids. Her house was always the weird smelly house, and her car was the one place where you rolled down the windows in 30-degree weather. And you can't just tell her about this fantastic new deodorant that smells like violets and sunshine, because the Smelly Friend's smell transcends hygiene. She is an olfactory amalgam of odd cooking habits, a laissez-faire approach to laundry, an aversion to scented shampoos, and something one might call "weird girl whiff." You tend to overcompensate when you hang out, leading your other friends or boyfriend to ponder aloud when Clinique Happy started coming in gallon jugs.

WHAT TO DO

Since you're never going to broach the subject,
Febreeze and bear it.

the klepto friend

HABITAT: Department stores, candy aisle, jail

IDENTIFYING CHARACTERISTICS: Shopping bags, nimble fingers, guilty grimace

PRO: Gives spectacular birthday presents

CON: They still have the security tags on them

CATCHPHRASE: "I'm just looking."

The Klepto Friend lives for the five-finger discount. A thousand-dollar silk scarf, drug store lipstick, her mom's Percocet—it really doesn't matter. She sees something, she wants it, she nabs it, and most of the time she doesn't get caught. You could examine her plight with earnest concern, discussing her problem with your other friends and postulating that she's "addicted to the rush" of stealing; but frankly she derives a little too much pleasure from her new Marc Jacobs clutch to provoke much sympathy. Shopping with her is a particularly harrowing experience, as you watch her slip into the swimwear or jewelry department and wait nervously for her to return, flushed and jubilant. You want to tell her that most of us got over the thrills of petty larceny in sixth grade, but you know she'll just tell you to relax and say something unintelligible about how it's a "victimless crime." Keep talkin', Winona.

WHAT TO DO

Cease shopping with her, which, in the Klepto Friend's case, means ceasing the friendship.

the backstabby friend

HABITAT: Behind your back

IDENTIFYING CHARACTERISTICS: Dark denim, musky perfume, air kisses

PRO: Mysterious and seemingly discreet

CON: Total bitch!

CATCHPHRASE: "No offense, but . . ."

This friend is the textbook definition of "Frenemy." You work together, but she kisses far more upper-management ass, and therefore is swiftly promoted. Or you have "friends in common"—and one of them happens to be your boyfriend. She gets you on board by seeming really invested in your friendship, but eventually you see she has ulterior motives. This girl is threatened by you—your looks, your charm, your position in work or in romance—and she responds with underhanded scheming. She's the queen of faux compliments ("You must have had a fun weekend . . . you look exhausted!") and will stop at nothing to take you down, cultivating neutral parties who might side against you. Sound like grade school all over again? It is! Backstabby is the grownup equivalent of the mean girl by the lockers who compliments your backpack and then makes a gagging motion as you walk away. Avoid!

WHAT TO DO

Change your e-mail, block her IM . . . in fact, it might be time for a career change. We hear the Trappist monks just opened a women's branch.

126

ill-gotten
corner office

mysterious and
seemingly discreet expression

air
kisses

musky
perfume

dark denim

acknowledgments

I would like to thank Maya Rock at Writers House for her ideas, tenacity, and pull-no-punches feedback. My sincere gratitude to Mindy Brown and Margaret McGuire at Quirk Books, whose wit and editing acumen know no bounds, as well as to Quirk's resident marketing geniuses Melissa Monachello and Lacey Soslow. Love and thanks to Pam, Jim, and Marylou Bradley, Sarah and Frank Wagner, and to Amy Olsson, Laura Mulloy, Jaime Byrd, and my other great friends who inspired this book (the nice parts!). And finally, thank you to my wonderful husband, Andrew, for his encouragement, prodigious editor's eye, and unflagging good humor.

HEATHER WAGNER is a writer based in New York. Her work has been published in *Travel & Leisure*, *Domino*, *Dwell*, the *UTNE Reader*, *SOMA*, and *Plenty*. She is currently a copywriter at *ELLE*.